Acknowledgments

This book is the fruit of nearly three decades of classroom teaching at Mannes School of Music–The New School. In these years, I have been continually challenged and inspired by my many extraordinary students. As with any book covering such a broad topic, I have benefited immeasurably from the wisdom of others. From those who preceded me, I received my spirit of inquiry and the sense of the essential dramatic nature of music from my mentor, Joan Brown. This approach was confirmed and refined by my work with Jacqueline DuPré as well as vocal pedagogues Randy Mickelson and Shirlee Emmons. I have relied on the wisdom and memory of my friends and colleagues Will Berger, Lydia Brown, Clarice Carter, Will Crutchfield, John Fiore, Graham Johnson, Eugene Kohn, Judith Malafronte, Fred Plotkin, Craig Rutenberg, Prof. Domna Stanton, and Jonathan Ziegler, without whom this volume would contain far more inaccuracies. Francis Keeping has been indispensable in all musical and Italian matters. I would like to thank Leon Major for the inspiration that I received from his complementary volume *The Empty Voice*, published by Amadeus Press. Without the enthusiastic assistance of Greg Sigman, the assistant director, Research and Instructional Services, at The New School Libraries, this book would have taken many more years to complete. My editor, Robert Levine, is responsible for the book's readability and intelligibility, and my husband, Lewis Jacobsen, is responsible for maintaining my sanity as I continually take on more than I ought.

Thank you all.

Kate Veale.

Beyond the Aria: Artistic Self-Empowerment for the Classical Singer

Why You Want It, Why You've Been
Denied It, and How to Achieve It

Neal Goren

AMADEUS PRESS

Lanham • Boulder • New York • London

Published by Amadeus Press
An imprint of The Rowman & Littlefield Publishing Group, Inc.
4501 Forbes Boulevard, Suite 200, Lanham, Maryland 20706
www.rowman.com

6 Tinworth Street, London SE11 5AL, United Kingdom

British Library Cataloguing in Publication Information Available

Library of Congress Cataloging-in-Publication Data

Names: Goren, Neal, author.
Title: Beyond the aria: Artistic self-empowerment for the classical singer
: why you want it, why you've been denied it, and how to achieve it /
Neal Goren.
Other titles: Artistic self-empowerment for the classical singer
Description: Lanham : Amadeus Press, 2020. | Includes bibliographical
references and index. | Summary: "This book will help singers develop an
inquisitive and analytical mindset about the artistic details found in
the scores being studied. Neal Goren helps singers feel musically
empowered to make and discuss their own valid artistic choices, deriving
greater satisfaction from their performances while making themselves
more employable"— Provided by publisher.
Identifiers: LCCN 2020038834 (print) | LCCN 2020038835 (ebook) | ISBN
9781538137932 (paperback) | ISBN 9781538137949 (epub)
Subjects: LCSH: Singing—Interpretation (Phrasing, dynamics, etc.) | Vocal
music—Interpretation (Phrasing, dynamics, etc.) |
Operas—Interpretation (Phrasing, dynamics, etc.) | Singing—Vocational
guidance.
Classification: LCC MT892 .G67 2020 (print) | LCC MT892 (ebook) | DDC
782.1/143—dc23
LC record available at https://lccn.loc.gov/2020038834
LC ebook record available at https://lccn.loc.gov/2020038835

Contents

Introduction

WHY YOU WANT ARTISTIC SELF-EMPOWERMENT

You, presumably, are an aspiring singer, whether still in music school or chasing after a (better) career as a singer. At every level of your training and professional engagements, you have, most likely, been treated with condescension by everyone around you (save your fellow singers, with whom you have been sharing the boat). Presumably, you have found this behavior to be offensive at best and infuriating at worst. Let's look at where this attitude originates.

By the age at which you began taking voice lessons, probably in your teens or later, your instrumentalist counterparts had been studying music for ten years or more. In those years, they have acquired not only a level of technical accomplishment, but also a musical proficiency: an understanding of how musical compositions are constructed and how the language of music developed. You, on the contrary, have spent your comparatively few years in the voice studio learning how to sing, to the exclusion of everything else. This is because mastering the art of singing is much more difficult than mastering an instrument. As you know all too well, your instrument is yourself, and mastering oneself is a never-ending challenge. Then there's the fact that your instrument is incredibly fragile and is at the mercy of hundreds of variables, some of which you can control and many that you cannot. And perhaps most significantly, instrumentalists are able to observe their mechanism while they play, while yours is hidden from sight and can only be perceived when abusing your instrument.

The window for entry into a singing career is brief. When you take this into consideration, along with the fact that vocal training cannot begin until you have a certain physical maturity without damaging your instrument, you cannot help but see that your potential training period is incredibly compressed compared to that of instrumentalists. Yes, instrumentalists have it far easier than you, yet they have the nerve to be condescending.

This is all because they have had the time to learn about music while they have been acquiring their less-demanding technical skills. If they have been lucky, their teachers have given them a grounding in harmony and musical structure, and virtually all have had the opportunity to learn how to think and talk about music. The instrumentalists have acquired the currency to join the club whose entrance is policed by those who have likewise been trained to speak the same language of music as their colleagues. Singers like yourself are not given the training to join that club and are left at the door, because your instrument, your voice, takes such immense skill to master, and you have so little time to master it.

Because you have most likely not learned this lingo, instrumentalists and conductors (who generally come from the rank of instrumentalists) tend to prejudge singers as being less intelligent than their own kind. This judgment is based on ignorance and short-sightedness, as are most prejudices. The fact remains that not only must you master an instrument that is infinitely more difficult to master than theirs, but you must memorize nearly all your music (which they rarely are called upon to do). Plus, your music requires a working knowledge of foreign languages, sometimes as many as five in one performance. What may be the greatest challenge of all is that you are generally required to move while singing exquisitely in a foreign language, and to move out of synch—i.e., "naturally"—with the music. The skill set required of singers is akin to performing surgery while on roller skates.

Considering all the various skills you've had to master in order to perform anything as a singer, it is actually a comparatively easy matter to acquire the lingo to give you entrance to the club. This can be achieved by developing an inquisitive and analytical approach to your music, informed by knowledge of some basic performance practice guidelines. That's all it takes. Starting with a spirit of joyful inquiry and then following the methodology I outline in the following chapters, your explorations will flower into a number of essential results. It will earn you respect from those whose respect you need: namely, the conductors and stage directors with whom you collaborate. It will also empower you to make intelligent, valid decisions about your musical interpretations. And it will give you a way to build the characters you inhabit that can only be judged to be valid, as it will emanate from the text and the music. And finally, it will result in you becoming a better artist, to be acknowledged as an artist in your own right, and to accrue the benefits that artists receive.

Learning what questions to ask yourself about the scores you study can have significant concrete results, which far outweigh the difficulty of pondering those questions. Firstly, you will be given respect as a musician by your instrumentalist friends. Secondly, you will be given respect by your conductor and given permission to dialogue as an equal about the music you are making together: no longer a puppet, but a partner. This will not only make you feel better, but it will make your conductor want to rehire you, because making music with equals is far more gratifying than collaborating with someone you consider to be your inferior.

Surely you have noticed that in each generation there are a handful of singers whose calendar of engagements is full, but whose instrument or technique may not merit this success. I would venture to say that these singers have learned what it takes to be considered artist-singers, versus the far more common puppet-singers.

Because your art is the vocal art, you need to learn specifically how conductors, stage directors, and even your instrumentalist collaborators speak about the music you are working on together in order to be taken seriously by them. While this may seem like a shallow goal, the process by which you attain this skill will enrich your performances and your studies. The actual goal is to make you a better artist, and the secondary goal is to be acknowledged as such.

This book can teach you to talk the language of conductors, the language of stage directors, and the language of instrumentalists (three different, but related, languages) that will consequently render you more desirable and employable in today's highly competitive job market.

Do not forget that musical preparation is vital: More than the occasional musical mistake will result in you being judged a poseur who talks a good game but cannot deliver! What you consider to be adequate preparation for a gig is likely to be considered inadequate by your conductor and stage director. If you consider yourself overprepared, then you are probably hitting the right mark. Leontyne Price asserted that she had to arrive at rehearsals better prepared than any of her colleagues in order to be perceived as adequately prepared. This was a gift in disguise, and it certainly helped establish and confirm her superstar status. Follow her example!

WHY YOU HAVE BEEN DENIED IT

While this title implies that there exists a conspiracy to deny you musical self-empowerment, I have seen no evidence that such a conspiracy actually exists.

That said, you have been denied musical self-empowerment, in spite of the ease of its acquisition. Instrumentalists generally receive the tools for self-empowerment from their teachers, but I have rarely encountered voice teachers who impart that information to their students. The reasons for this I believe are twofold.

First of all, they may not know themselves. In this regard, the situation has not changed perceptibly in the last few decades: Their teachers also did not know and therefore did not pass the necessary information on to your teacher.

Second of all, if they do know, they are too busy teaching you how to sing to take the time for anything else. It has been a hundred years since singers with great potential had daily lessons with their teachers. That was the norm then. Now, a single weekly lesson is the norm, and your teacher has to fit in a week's worth of instruction into that single hour. Besides, for all musical concerns, you probably go to a coach.

Having worked as a coach concurrently with my work as a conductor, collaborative pianist, and educator for decades, I can accurately speak for my coach colleagues.

A likely reason is that they may think that you enjoy being spoon-fed, as many people do. Perhaps they judge you as incurious or even lazy or spoiled. You might consider some soul-searching to assess why they may have gotten that idea, or you could simply ask.

Another reason is that they may like being seen as the authority and are unwilling to give up that role by teaching you to take over for yourself what you have been relying on them for. Many coaches have a deep psychological need to be admired, depended upon, or even worshiped, and you are filling that need. If that describes your relationship, they should be paying you, not vice versa.

The possibility also exists that, like your teacher, your coach (or coaches) may not possess this information, or they are too lazy themselves to pass it on. Our industry is teeming with charlatans. Or perhaps helping you learn your music takes up all the time they have allotted to you.

Which leads us to what is the principal reason why coaches do not teach you musical self-empowerment—and that reason is that your coaches are afraid of losing their income. While you may feel that your relationship with your coach is based on caring and sharing, I can assure you that they need to make a living, and you are an integral part of that. If coaches were to teach musical self-empowerment to all their clients, they fear (either consciously or unconsciously) that they would become superfluous.

Singers, I do not want to give you the idea that upon acquiring the skills of musical self-empowerment and embracing your power, you will be paying out less money for musical preparation. This is not the case. You will instead apportion your investments differently and more wisely. You will continue to spend your money on répétiteurs to routine your music and correct any musical mistakes that may have crept in. It is a fact that répétiteurs generally charge approximately 50 percent of what coaches charge, so you may find yourself spending less money on coaches, or you may choose to visit the répétiteur more than you have been doing, so you can arrive at rehearsal feeling fully confident in your level of musical preparation. If your musical skills are less than brilliant, the best possible investment would be lessons in sight-singing and ear training, which will also empower you further and save you significant money in both the long and the short term. (Even the best music conservatories have been notably reducing these requirements, thereby shirking their responsibility to educate you where it would benefit you the most.) You will continue to pay specialized diction coaches as needed, and you will continue to visit your voice teacher.

Your musical coach will serve a narrower role than (s)he has up until now. Your coach will become your partner in musical exploration, brainstorming along with you to discover what the music is trying to communicate and experimenting with ways to achieve it. I would like to illustrate the singer-coach relationship at the highest level: My most fulfilling musical relationship was with legendary soprano Leontyne Price. In the hundreds of hours we spent rehearing music we'd already performed many times together, we would experiment with different ways to express the music, and experiment with the boundaries (both upper and lower) of emotionality for each song, so that our performances could be spontaneous, creative experiences. Our unspoken goal was not to decide and set an ultimate performance of a song or aria, but to set parameters for ourselves in which we could create the music and characters in the concerts, as it would seem appropriate to us and the audience at the moment.

Likewise, your sessions with your acting coach would be devoted to sharing ideas and trying valid interpretations on for size.

We will now begin to explore how to achieve musical self-empowerment.

NOTE TO COACH-ACCOMPANISTS AND ASPIRING OPERA CONDUCTORS

I can assure you that, should singers take up the challenge to empower themselves artistically, you will not lose your client base, but you should be aware that your role would change. Instead of telling your clients what to do and where to do it, you would begin having serious, high-level discussions about the composers' and librettists' intentions and how to execute them. You would certainly continue to share the musical traditions that exist for any work studied, but you would explore the reasons why the traditions developed and, in partnership with your clients, discuss whether those reasons are valid or even proper. This would require a higher level of expertise and preparation than what you may currently provide, but the artistic rewards will be well worth the effort.

Should more of your clients challenge themselves to become musicians by using the tools for artistic self-empowerment provided in the upcoming chapters, you are likely to lose dependents and worshipers; but if you are honest with yourselves, the promise of being worshiped is not what drew you to this profession in the first place. If it is, there are professions that can satisfy that emotional need far better than music. Emotional dependency and lack of boundaries were inappropriate aspects of the singer/coach-accompanist relationship that I could not extricate myself from soon enough.

I remember a famous colleague of mine explaining that the singer/coach-accompanist relationship is unhealthy by definition. It is a relationship that requires the coach-accompanist to be an authority in all aspects of musical preparation and performance, yet to expect no credit and only highly disproportionate remuneration for his unstinting efforts. An imbalance of power defines the relationship. In the studio, the coach-accompanist holds all the power, yet on the recital platform the roles are totally reversed. I was told by my colleague that the most successful coach-accompanists possess personalities like Uriah Heep in Charles Dickens's *David Copperfield*. Heep exhibits an oily obsequiousness to everyone with whom he comes in contact, while harboring an unshakeable sense of superiority. While I know of no coach-accompanist who, like Heep, wishes for the downfall of his employers, I have unfortunately known far too many who harbor resentment toward their charges.

It is possible that some of your clients already have developed artistic self-empowerment through their own perspicacity. If so, you have already learned to interact with them differently from your other clients, and it is likely that you look forward to their visits. If you do not relish the nature of your interaction with them and the additional preparation that is required of you to satisfy their musical inquiries, perhaps you would be happier by defining yourself as a répétiteur, whose job is clearly circumscribed. As a coach-accompanist for the artistically empowered singer, you will find yourself intellectually challenged every day in untold ways. And you will find yourself not having all the answers, because the questions you will discuss will be challenging and often unanswerable. You must make peace with not being seen as a great authority in all things musical (as another well-known colleague of mine used to enjoy the epithet of "immenso Phta" after the god in Verdi's Aida), but rather as a partner in inquiry and, if you are lucky, as a friend.

I

Tools for Musical Self-Empowerment

Know Where You're Going

It's best to think of yourself as a musical tour guide.

You are presenting a piece of music to an audience, guiding them through the music to hear it as you think it should be heard and understood. To realize an effective and valid performance of any chosen composition, you must first deconstruct it and make conscious, specific, and informed decisions about the music and text in order to best communicate its contents, both superficial and underlying. Like a tour guide, it is up to you to curate and prioritize the audience's experience, always keeping in mind the music's destination, much as a tour guide may make as many stops as are important on the way to the ultimate geographical goal, never forgetting that you must arrive by a certain hour.

Every successful instrumentalist and conductor I have encountered has analyzed every phrase of every composition they present. The first step is for the interpreter to determine where each phrase begins and ends. Since composers of abstract music are rarely punctilious when notating phrase lengths for those instruments for which an intake of breath is not required to initiate the sound, such as strings and keyboard instruments, it is up to the interpreter to decide how to carve up a phrase that may be notated as being pages in length (e.g., the opening of the Adagio assai of the Ravel G major Piano Concerto or the Adagio of Beethoven's Symphony No. 4, or any Chopin Nocturne). Singers may be amused to learn that these same conductors and instrumentalists who hold them in low musical esteem, when confronted with extremely long phrases, base their determination of phrase lengths on the duration of their breath when attempting to sing the tune.

The next step is to define the goal of each phrase in order for its performance to sound natural and organic. Generally, each phase moves toward the moment of greatest harmonic tension, then the tension is dissipated (sometimes immediately, sometimes more slowly and deliberately) to its resolution. The movement toward the moment of greatest harmonic tension is not necessarily experienced as an accelerando; rather it is felt as a magnetic attraction and pull. Whatever spots one lingers over en route must increase the magnetic pull toward the goal, rather than dissipating it. I heard the great conductor/pianist Daniel Barenboim comparing a fermata to a river being dammed as it approaches a waterfall, with its pressure continually mounting until it either overflows its walls or breaks through the dam, rushing toward its fall to earth. This simile vividly captures the force of the musical phrase toward its goal and eventual resolution.

Singers should feel no shame in drawing arrows into their music in order to visualize the goal of each phrase. Without feeling the attraction toward the goal, held high notes strike the listener as unmusical and self-indulgent. On the other hand, if the performer feels the pull toward the goal, the held high notes are experienced by the listener as thrilling, visceral events.

Identifying the goal of each phrase of vocal music is a far easier prospect than it is for abstract music because the text nearly always provides you with clues. We must begin with the text because that is where the composers began, and the text is invariably what inspired their music.

In Italian music, the goal of each phrase is nearly always the second-to-last syllable of the phrase (e.g., "Come scoglio immoto resta"). The exception to this penultimate syllable principle for Italian repertoire is not so much an exception as a poetic modification: the librettists often truncated that final syllable for reasons of syllabification, leaving off its final vowel (like amor for amore or cor for core), which results in the musical phrase being pulled toward what is now the final syllable, rather than the penultimate (aka parola tronca). Implementation of this principle is of paramount importance in the interpretation of all Italian vocal music, but especially in that of Mozart, as we will explore in a later chapter, and it exemplifies the difference between what is judged to be a stylistic, musical interpretation and an unmusical, egocentric one.

And what about other commonly sung languages? There exists a common misconception about the French language, namely that it does not contain accented or unaccented syllables. Anyone with even a passing acquaintance with the language knows that this is not accurate. If this were the case, French composers would have been forced to set their language exclusively as free recitative. Like their Italian counterparts, the French composers placed the goal of their phrases as the penultimate syllable of the phrase when the final syllable is followed by the sung schwa, and this penultimate syllable is generally a chord of tension, which is followed by its resolution. Think of Faust's aria: "Salut! Demeure chaste et pure . . . d'une âme innocente et divine" or Don José's "La fleur que tu m'avais jetée . . ." When there is no sung schwa following the final syllable, the underlying chord can either be one of tension or of resolution. In either case, the goal of the phrase is its end.

The German language has even stronger word accents than English, and you will generally find that the musical phrase also moves toward the final accented syllable of the phrase, but unlike the Italian repertoire, this occurs, as often as not, at a moment of harmonic resolution rather than tension (Pamina's aria, "Ach, ich fühl's, es ist verschwunden").

What makes the vocal writing of Wagner, Weber, Bach, and, to a lesser extent, most of the great Lieder composers particularly difficult to execute is that the final accented syllable of the phrase is rarely set on a resonant area within a singer's range. That is why the German repertoire is commonly considered to be written instrumentally. Much of the Lieder repertoire concerns itself with sadness and sorrowful emotions, whose general melodic shape is downward into the less resonant area of the voice. The significant exception is R. Strauss, whose understanding of how voices work was second to none. The key to a successful performance of all music is to feel the direction of the phrase, regardless of where it sits in your voice or where the rest of the phrase lies.

English is no different. Though many composers have not been as adept at setting English, the composers for whom English is their first language uniformly set the texts with the end being the goal. Though Carlisle Floyd appears to set the phrase "Ain't it a pretty night" as having "pretty" as its apex, the phrase only makes musical sense if it moves toward "night," regardless of how long one lingers on "pretty." Likewise, Stravinsky violates the natural English prosody at every turn in "The Rake's Progress." If you allow Stravinsky's musical lines to seduce you away from singing the text toward the end of the phrase, it will render the text incomprehensible (which is challenging enough to the audience even when fully understood). Therefore, if the tenor directs Tom's phrase "... my wit ready, my heart light" toward "light" rather than "heart" (as Stravinsky seems to have set it), the phrase will hold a chance at being understood, both textually and musically. Handel, too, presents challenges to the singer in his English operas and oratorios. When Jupiter sings "... shall crowd into a shade" at the end of the A section of "Where e'er you walk," the phrase needs to be directed toward "shade," in spite of it commencing on a much higher note, in order for it to sound musical and natural.

I am not suggesting that one must relentlessly drive every phrase toward its goal, but without a defined goal, the music only meanders and is rendered meaningless to the audience. Tour guides do stop along the way to show off beguiling sights, knowing where they are ultimately headed. Likewise, the music's phrase directionality can be violated artfully and with great effect, provided that it is a conscious decision and is the exception rather than the rule. Indeed, it is the exception that can define the validity of the rule, but your choices must come from an intimate knowledge of the language, the music, and the interaction of the language and the music. I have never ceased to be moved, touched, and astonished by English tenor Laurence Dale's incomparably stylish interpretations of French arias in his 1988 recording, which has become the standard for this repertoire. Dale draws attention to syllables that most singers throw away, and this results in surprising textural or rhythmic emphases that are nonetheless valid. For example, in "Salut! Demeure chaste et pure" from *Faust*, Dale sings, "Ô Marguerite! A tes pieds me voici!" instead of the expected "Ô Marguerite! A tes pieds me voici!" and the result is deeply moving.

In atonal music, with its often highly angular vocal writing, it is particularly important that the direction of the phrase, based on the goal of its text (since the music often does not give any directional clues), be accorded particular attention in order to make the music comprehensible to an audience.

You might wonder why every phrase drives toward its conclusion and every musical phrase drives toward the cadence. The answer is very simple: Try shaping any spoken phrase toward its middle rather than its end. There is a lack of tension, a limpness, after its apex, which gives an impression of an apologetic delivery and causes the listener to lose interest midstream. Allowing the listener to lose interest is the greatest sin in musical performance, and it must be avoided at all costs.

Now the fun really begins!

By prioritizing the arrival points that you have already identified, you are developing and committing to a concept of the music's architecture and shaping an interpretation. Most importantly, you will be constructing a topographical emotional map of the music, which will prepare you for your duties as the tour guide of the music. This prioritization will serve as the map you follow when you serve as the tour guide for your audience.

There is no right and wrong in this decision-making process; Again, let yourself be guided by the music and the text when prioritizing the arrival points. A quick glance at the music can usually lead you directly to your musical climaxes, identifiable by the dynamics (the loudest or softest point of the music) and the range (the highest or lowest notes in the vocal part). This will usually be mirrored by extreme emotionality in the text, even if it is an exclamation such as "ah!" or "oh!" The emotion can either be extrovert or introvert, but it should be a strong emotion. A composer would never bother to write music that communicates a weak, limp emotion. Always remember that your principal job is to communicate emotion, and that is the sole reason for your acquisition of vocal technique. In the words of Renata Scotto: "Words shape everything. The voice must be secure, of course; and the technique must be clean. But when I am onstage I take for granted the vocal equipment through concentration. Then it is the words that shape the voice and color its sound. Every word counts in a great opera."[1]

Considering the text alone may make it difficult to identify where the climaxes occur, especially when the same text is repeated many, many times. A clear (actually unclear) example occurs in the aria "Mi tradì," from *Don Giovanni*, in which Donna Elvira is attempting to process her conflicting emotions toward her seducer. In this aria, she sings, "Provo ancor per lui pietà" ("I still feel pity for him") six times, plus the latter part of the phrase ("per lui pietà") ("pity for him") an additional three times. In order to prioritize these repetitions, you must begin by considering what emotions might cause her to obsessively repeat this phrase. Some of these might be general anger toward Don Giovanni, anger for her repeated humiliation by Don Giovanni, anger at herself for still loving him in spite of everything, and self-disgust for remaining in love with someone who has repeatedly proven himself to be thoroughly despicable. You should then consider the relative intensity of each emotion and consider how you want to order them, whether as a kaleidoscopic schizoid succession of emotions or building to a full-fledged mad scene. This aria can accommodate either interpretation.

It is not necessary that these motivations be fixed, only that they be fully considered. It is likely that you will decide that one particular musical figure suits one motivation best. What you choose is entirely up to you, the singer. You may feel that Donna Elvira's self-disgust may best be depicted in a high-lying melismatic phrase with many A flats, or you may feel that her debasement is best mirrored by a low phrase that dips down into chest voice, or vice versa. In any case, your choice will be repeated in every subsequent performance you give, either consciously or unconsciously. The way you choose to order these emotions is your artistic interpretation, which should be experienced by you and your audience as an emotional topographical map. This map is a distillation of the work's essence, according to you. You can pick and choose from your wardrobe of possible motivations in the course of the performance, without fear of making this character seem too overwrought, which would be virtually impossible. Considered, informed spontaneity is a good thing. Unconsidered spontaneity is never good and is perceived by the audience and conductor as undisciplined and egocentric.

2

Text Analysis and Expression Marks

Where to Begin

The first step toward musical self-empowerment is to imagine yourself to be the composer, deciding how to set a received text. In order to do that, you must understand the text literally. If it is not written in your native tongue, begin by translating it word-by-word, then puzzle out its colloquial meaning. Be sure to write both in your score, in pencil (you may choose to refine your translation over time). If it is an opera by a standard composer, the late, great character tenor and language coach of the Metropolitan Opera, Nico Castel, has done the work for you; his books of libretto translations are readily available and highly recommended. If the work is less standard but has been recorded commercially, complete libretti with English translations are generally included along with the recording; hundreds are available online. Otherwise, do your best with the dictionary and find a native speaker of the foreign language to help you formulate your colloquial translation.

Once your colloquial translation (based on the literal translation) has been completed, you must learn its context. If you are studying an opera aria, you need to discover, at the very least, what situation has occurred that would compel the character to sing that text. Arias are composed to actively communicate a character's emotion in direct response to a condition, and it is your job to consider as many emotional possibilities as you can imagine that might prompt such a response. Then identify for yourself which emotion you would choose in response to the situation if you were the composer.

Now return to the text and postulate for yourself which emotion the librettist seems to have chosen for the character to sing about. I write seems to because both opera characters and real people do not always say what they mean. They may be lying to themselves, perhaps because they find the truth too painful. They may be lying to whomever they are speaking, for any number of reasons. They may be trying to convince themselves or others of something that may not be true or that may be difficult to accept. Only by listening to the music can you discern whether the music is supporting the text or contradicting it. If it is the latter, come up with reasons why the character is saying what he or she is saying, in contrast to what the music is telling you. After having made conclusions about your character based on the text and possible subtexts, you must ascertain whether the music will support your characterization. If not, you must have the courage to start over and choose another characterization that the music will support.

In developing your character, it is of the utmost importance to decide where you think each new thought occurs in the text. Once you have made that determination, see if your assessment is mirrored in the music, or whether the composer made a different determination. If the composer has chosen a different interpretation of where the character's thoughts begin and end, you must consider why. Sometimes the composer will put a long pause in the middle of what you interpret to be the same thought in the text. This could mean many things; perhaps the character is formulating her thoughts as she goes, the character may be pausing to consider the best way to express her thoughts, the character may be pausing to assess whether what she is saying is indeed the case, or perhaps what follows the pause is not part of the preceding thought, but a new thought altogether. The consideration of where the character's new thoughts begin is paramount in recitatives, and it is the interpretive choice on which all others will be based.

If the character repeats a portion of the text, you must decide why. The character may be processing the emotion, or incredulous, or trying to comprehend; the possibilities are endless. You must entertain as many options as you can and choose what fits your idea of the character (as evinced by the music) best. Please refer back to "Know Where You're

Going" for a discussion of the numerous textual repeats in Donna Elvira's aria, Mi tradì, from Don Giovanni.

The next question in your textual/musical analysis is how the character gets from one thought to the next. Often, one thought mutates into the next in an organic, obvious manner. Equally often, the connection between one thought and the next is not so obvious. In these cases, you must decide for yourself what the connection is for the character between thought A and thought B. By doing so, you will begin to know the character intimately and make her your own. Emotional specificity can beget a convincing performance, whereas emotional vagueness guarantees an unconvincing one.

Now that you have considered the text, its context, and its possible subtexts, it is time to begin your musical/emotional analysis of the music. In chapter 13, you will find six sample analyses that you can use as paradigms to help guide your inquiry into your own repertoire.

EXPRESSION MARKS

I would encourage you to consider the expressive content of all expression marks found in your music. Executing them slavishly means only that you have followed the letter of the score while perhaps ignoring its spirit.

Please permit me a digression here. After college, I managed to convince the great cellist Jacqueline Du Pré to take me on as her only piano student. When I first requested this of her, she was skeptical; she responded that she did not play the piano and did not know what she had to offer me. I explained that it was her approach to music-making that was of interest to me. She was perhaps the most expressive performer in the latter half of the twentieth century, and I wanted a part of it. When she understood what I wanted from her, she proved eager to explore this within herself and to pass it on.

At one lesson, I was playing a standard solo piano piece: I believe it was a late Beethoven sonata. I recall her stopping me at one point and asking me why I was playing softly. I responded that in the score the passage was marked piano, and I was doing what the composer was asking of me. She then asked me to play the passage forte, which I did. Upon hearing this, her response was "at this point in your life, you are only able to communicate this passage forte. Until you can discover an emotional reason to play it piano, you must play it forte. The spirit of the music must always take precedence over the letter." This latter sentence proved, for me, to be the essence of her musical sensibility: Define for yourself what the composer is trying to communicate, and communicate it! Discovering what the composer is trying to communicate is the subject of this book.

Here are some commonly encountered expression marks, along with questions you should ask yourself about them, and possible expressive content that you might consider.

The first expression mark you will encounter in any piece of music is its tempo. After studying the text, ask yourself why the composer chose that tempo. This consideration is most interesting and exciting for you as an artist when the composer has made a counterintuitive choice. It is incumbent upon you to find an emotional reason that you can communicate for the seemingly odd tempo choice.

The same goes for dynamics, as in the Jacqueline Du Pré story that I just related. Jackie had the wisdom to realize that I was not yet able to justify Beethoven's specific dynamic. She did not let me off the hook: I had to keep searching for a reason that resonated within me that I could communicate both the letter and the spirit of the music. I had an obligation to both the composer and to the audience, and it was necessary for me to satisfy both.

I have had the good fortune to work with great living composers from Gian-Carlo Menotti to Nico Muhly to David Hertzberg. In each instance, the composer was eager to make changes to accommodate a performer's strong expressive conviction. Another story: I was preparing to conduct the world premiere of Nico Muhly's seminal chamber opera, Dark Sisters. Nearing the dress rehearsal, I approached him to discuss whether I was executing some specific musical details to his satisfaction. Perhaps exasperated with my compulsion for exactitude and my desire to please, he responded, "This is no longer my opera, it is yours. You must own it and do what you think best from now on."

Rests, the absence of sound, are perhaps your single greatest opportunity for expression. The contemporary Estonian composer Arvo Pärt said that sometimes the most beautiful part of a composition is the space between the notes. Think about that! There are countless reasons for a rest beyond the mere need for a breath. It can be a moment to consider a thought, to assess a feeling, to let an emotion percolate, or even to prepare an emotional catharsis. Consider the length of the rest and what is happening in the character's thought process over that amount of time. The greatest master of breaths one could ever hope to encounter was Jessye Norman. I would encourage you to become acquainted with her art, and in particular, the incomparable expressivity of her rests.

Often an articulation mirrors an inner emotional state. Staccatti often serve as a stand-in for laughter They can express giddiness (though rarely in men or noblewomen). Or they can express madness or vehemence. (In Mozart's arias for Donna Anna and the Queen of the Night, for example, either option can communicate itself effectively.) As for legato singing, it generally suggests a sense of poise and emotional control. Legato singing is generally the default mode for singers because it promotes good technical habits. But is it appropriate emotionally as a default?

Phrase lengths should be considered. Just as a sentence can be interrupted by numerous commas and clauses (a sentence in Proust can run on for pages!), a single sung thought can be broken by a dozen rests, for reasons both emotional and practical. Always analyze where one thought begins and ends, and let that analysis communicate itself with clarity. It will shape your impression of how the character thinks and expresses himself/herself.

Legato for singers is something different than legato for instrumentalists! It took me many years to realize this fact, and I regret any misinformation that I spread. If you push too much air to tie one note to the next, you will hyper-phonate, overstressing your vocal mechanism, and your words will be incomprehensible. Effecting the *impression* of legato for a singer must be considered in relation to the enunciation of the text. As a general rule, the more syllables per square inch (like in *secco* recitative), the more buoyant your air must be. In these instances, a supported speaking on pitch will give a much better impression of legato than a pressurized vocal line. Your vocal health must be treasured. This vocal revelation was shared with me by the late, great music critics and vocal enthusiasts Andrew Porter and Desmond Shawe-Taylor over sherry in

London. As a young pianist, I did not know what they meant, but I do now and am eager to pass this wisdom on.

For singers, **two-note phrases** rarely imply a staccato on the second note, contrary to what you may have been taught. If a composer wants this effect from the singer, it is nearly always notated with a staccato on the second note or a brief rest following it. I do not believe that Verdi actually wanted a hiccup effect in the two-note phrases in *Sempre libera*! It is best to think of a two-note phrase as a bowing marking transferred to the voice. In vocal music of the nineteenth century, if a two-note phrase is notated on a single syllable, it generally indicates a portamento should occur adjoining one note to the next. If accompanied by a diminuendo between the first and second note (whether ascending or descending), the effect is a sigh. Each of these effects must express an emotion, and it is up to you to choose the emotion and communicate it effectively.

Accents are particularly misunderstood by most singers. If a typical vocal line looks something like this dynamically:

with the volume of the phrase reaching its peak somewhere toward its middle, pianists and percussionists have no choice but to play an accent at the peak of the phrase as this:

In other words, to hit the note harder than the surrounding notes. This is an accent defined by its attack (notice the violence implied by the word). Its effect is aggressive and violent. When a singer executes an accent in this manner, you inevitably stress your throat unnecessarily. A healthier and easier way to execute an accent for a singer (or a wind player) is like this:

which results in a totally different, nonaggressive expression. Its execution is of a very sudden extreme diminuendo, followed immediately by a return to the dynamic shape of the phrase; in other words, it is defined not by the attack but by the decay. As evidence of the rightness of this execution, notice how closely an accent visually resembles a diminuendo: It is noted exactly the same, but in miniature. The effect of this execution of the accent is vulnerability, rather than aggression.

As for other accents that you will commonly encounter, the sforzando and the marcato are executed exactly the same as the example above, the difference being the speed and contrast of the diminuendo to the rest of the line.

For my ear, extended vibrato-less singing is hideous and disturbing. I would adapt Manuel Garcia's sentiment, "voix blanche, voix ouverte, voix horrible!" to read "voix blanche, voix non-vibrante, voix horrible!" I am not advocating for the wobble of a damaged instrument, but rather the free vibration of a healthy one. Withholding vibrato can admittedly cause an eerie special effect, which, used too frequently, loses its expressivity and generally results in flatness of pitch. To withhold vibrato, you must manipulate your instrument by tightening, which is never a good habit to encourage. It is an effect to be used sparingly and cautiously. I know that I am inviting invective here, but the vibrato-less singing demanded by many conductors of early and modern music results (to my ears) in an imposed, twisted emotional blankness. If one trains one's voice to be a perfect receptacle and communicator of emotion, why negate that goal by suppressing your instrument's freedom and ability to communicate?

3

Ornamentation and Recitative

To discuss ornamentation thoroughly would require an entire volume of its own. Here I would just like to set up some guidelines for singers as they explore this complex subject for themselves.

Firstly, and most importantly, the ornaments should augment the mood of the music that is to be ornamented and should never violate or change the essential mood. In order to achieve this, you must be able to articulate what you, in collaboration with the text and the music, are trying to communicate. One would never augment a mood of quiet contemplation as one would augment a mood of wild passion. Many moods are neither one thing nor the other, but are complex, often with an introverted hue and an extroverted one. Your ornaments can accentuate one aspect or another of the essential mood carried by the music and the text, but to do so effectively, you must know specifically what you are trying to achieve.

On a practical level, any ornaments you compose must align perfectly with the harmony, of course.

To this, I would add that awareness of stylistic practice is essential. One must not ornament Mozart as one ornaments Vivaldi or Donizetti. The best guidelines to follow are examples by the composers themselves or treatises that are contemporaneous with the composition you are ornamenting.

As a paradigm of Mozart ornamentation, for example, you might begin with Mozart's own ornamentation of his aria "Ah se a morir mi chiama" from Lucia Silla, which can be found in the appendix of the Bärenreiter edition of the complete opera. For additional guidance, you might turn to an ornamentation of Cherubino's famous aria "Voi che sapete" from *Le nozze di Figaro*, composed by Mozart's contemporary, Domenico Corri. To our ears, these examples are as elaborate and over-the-top as any ornamentation of Rossini as one is likely to encounter. It has been suggested that these examples were composed as examples of ornaments one might apply selectively, rather than in their entirety. We will never know. The days are over when Mozart's melodies were considered sacrosanct and inviolable. If your ornaments serve to augment the mood of the music and are executed within that spirit, they are likely to be received with appreciation rather than horror.

For authoritative information on ornamentation for Handel and his contemporaries, we will have to wait for the publication of Will Crutchfield's book on bel canto, which promises to deal extensively on ornamentation of Italian Baroque operatic repertoire.

In the case of Rossini and the *bel canto* composers, we are on firmer ground. One can begin by studying Rossini's own ornaments for "Di tanti palpiti" from *Tancredi* and the numerous examples he composed for his *Aureliano in Palmira*. One can turn to Manuel Garcia's treatises for additional exemplars (see the section titled "The *bel canto* composers" in chapter 4 of this volume). Again, one should begin with the premise that the ornaments should be in the service of augmenting the original mood that the composer intended to convey.

It is worth mentioning that there exist vocal showpieces that are intended to express nothing beyond evoking wonder and astonishment from the audience, such as Adolphe Adam's Variations on "Ah! vous dirai-je maman" (aka Twinkle, twinkle little star) and any number of Rossini arias, especially those he repurposed from other operas. These virtuoso vehicles can be ornamented limitlessly in order to increase the audience's wonder and astonishment. Any pretense of good taste can be freely ignored in these instances.

When executing the ornaments, I would strongly advise that you do not lose the forest for the trees. The little notes are not the point (except perhaps in the virtuoso showpieces). Do not ignore the direction of the phrases (see chapter 1: "Know Where You're Going") as that is what ultimately signals your musicianship to the listener.

Generally, ornamentation is inappropriate for music composed past the middle of the nineteenth century, when musical priorities shifted from the performer to the composer.

RECITATIVE

Recitative preparation presents you with your greatest artistic challenge and affords you your greatest opportunity for artistic expression, character building, and personal gratification. Legendary soprano Renata Scotto explained to me, "Recitative is the moment when the actor can make the audience understand the character." To this, I might add that recitative is when you have the best opportunity to construct and define your character in order to share it with your audience. Scotto continued, [when learning repertoire that contained recitative], "I would begin by building the character from learning and studying the recitative. Then I would study the music, relating it to the recitative, until both made a complete character."

Executing recitative convincingly requires more steps in the learning process than any other type of vocal music. I will present a methodology that I have developed over the years to accomplish a successful learning process for Italian recitative. The same process can be adapted to recitative in other languages as well. Throughout the process, keep in mind that the effect you want to achieve in recitative is text spoken and enacted on pitch, rather than sung. The latter would result in heavy, turgid, lugubrious recitative, which is certainly not what the composers had in mind.

Secco recitative

As with all other vocal music, begin with the text. Learn the plot to at least the beginning of the recitative. If you speak or read Italian well, translate any words you don't know, puzzle out the meaning of any stilted grammar, and write a loose translation above any confusing places. If you have some Italian experience (i.e., if you know some of the grammar but are not conversant), translate every word literally, write it above or below the printed Italian, plus a loose translation of anything confusing. (You may need to white-out the printed singing translation in order to have enough room.) Feel free to use any tools at your disposal: dictionary, translations (Nico Castel's are an invaluable resource), libretti from CDs, and any Italians you know. If you have no Italian language experience, try to get some immediately, at least enough so you recognize nouns and verbs. If you can't get your hand on a word-by-word translation, find an Italian—fast—to help you out. Warning: Disregard singing translations published in the scores. NB: The less Italian you know, the more help you'll need.

Now that you have done your preliminary work, you are ready to begin your analysis.

Next, analyze your character in relation to the words and situation. Consider the following: Is there a subtext? What is the character's mood? Try and understand the character fully and his/her reasons for saying these words. Whom is he/she speaking to? Does he/she mean what he/she is saying?

Go to the music, consider the composer's emphases, both pitch and duration. (Composers emphasize words or syllables in recitative by setting them in either extreme of a singer's vocal range. Furthermore, long notes receive more emphasis than short notes.) For now, ignore the actual pitches and rhythms notated.

Moving ahead, speak the translation, in character, in your native tongue out loud. Try to communicate the mood in speech. If possible, try to emphasize the same words in the same emphases as the composer has done. (This may not be possible in some languages—i.e., tone languages.) How does your characterization affect the tempo of delivery of each thought? This latter awareness is vitally important: Write your conclusions into the music.

You are now ready to repeat the above, but in Italian. Try a few different characterizations on for size and analyze your results.

Knowing that, in secco recitative, the 4/4 time signature is there for organizational purposes only. Analyze the rests written in music and the punctuation written in text. Decide which rests to keep and which to disregard, based on your results from the previous steps. These decisions should be made in light of where your character's thoughts begin and end. Rests separating thoughts generally make more sense than rests that lie within a thought. Experiment: Try different possibilities. This, too, is very important. In pencil, cross out those rests you feel would be omitted in speech.

Now speak the recitative aloud again in Italian, incorporating the decisions you have made thus far. Practice this until your delivery sounds like natural speech, and do not move on until you have achieved this.

You can now analyze the dialogue in relation to the other characters in the recitative. Should your entrance overlap their speech, or should you let time pass before responding? Why?

Now, finally, it's time to add the pitches. Be attentive to maintain the same tempi and essential delivery when singing as you did when speaking. In general, you would be better off thinking of delivering recitative as speaking on pitch, rather than singing (except in some accompanied recitative passages, which will be obvious). This may require you to use less air and a more buoyant air stream than you are accustomed to using. Adapt your technique to your musical conception: That's what it's for!

Be prepared to verbalize for harpsichordist (and conductor and director) what mood/characterization you're trying to achieve. Your harpsichordist can become your partner in achieving your artistic goals in recitative, or (s)he can actually prevent you from achieving them. Treasure your harpsichordists like the artistic collaborators you want them to be.

Many years ago, as a young aspiring coach-accompanist, I was invited to play and coach the recitatives for a concert performance of Mozart's *Mitridate* for the Mostly Mozart Festival in New York. At the recitative rehearsal, the singers were seated in a semicircle facing me and each other. All the of singers, with the exception of one, were young, aspiring artists hoping to make their mark in the industry. As we worked through the score, I found myself bringing up the musical issues discussed above with each aspiring singer, which many had never considered, while often fumbling for their notes. When we finally arrived at the music for Farnace, sung by veteran mezzo soprano Tatiana Troyanos, she stood up, closed her score, and preceded to tell me what mood or subtext she was aiming to achieve on each phrase, inviting me to aid her musically with my accompaniment. If the young singers did not feel chastened, they should have. Troyanos provided me with a lesson in artistic collaboration and all of us with a lesson in professionalism.

Recitativo stromentato, aka accompanied recitative

You need to know that conducting accompanied recitative presents the greatest technical challenge for conductors. Therefore, your goal should be to collaborate with your conductor on his/her terms in accompanied recitative to achieve a cohesive and convincing interpretation with your orchestra that can be accomplished seamlessly and without fear. What this means is that you will need to find out from your conductor exactly where you need to sing in rhythm and where you can be free rhythmically. You may need to adapt your interpretation to fit the musical necessities of the conductor and orchestra. If you are resistant or uncooperative, the performance will suffer, and you will never be hired by that conductor again. You can probably ascertain what those musical necessities will be in advance by imagining yourself to be the conductor, analyzing which measures can be performed rhythmically freely (no orchestra or only tremoli accompaniment) and which measures will probably need to be performed in time. You can then proceed to learn the free sections as you would *recitativi secchi*. Prepare the measured sections as you would the *secchi*, too, but in rhythm. Also analyze where your conductor will need your help by connecting visually, including all tempo changes, and practice doing this. Also consider which entrances and arrivals must happen in unison with the orchestra, and which might be postponed. Be aware that your conductor may have different ideas. In accompanied recitative, always defer to the needs of the conductor.

II

PERFORMANCE PRACTICE

4

Overview

Performance Practice

One must not assume that the way humans perceive musical emotion has been the same for the four hundred years since opera first came into being. Knowing to what extent the perception of emotion has changed in our lifetimes, we can only assume that the change in these four hundred years has been profound. For example, how people perceive men crying has, over time, evolved from (in ancient Greece) being a model for how heroic men should behave, to (in my youth) being a sign of unforgiveable weakness, to a sign of welcome vulnerability (now).[1]

It is therefore prudent to assume that what was seen as admirably expressive in past centuries will not be perceived that same way presently. Styles and tastes change, and we must be cognizant of our present sensibilities when performing for a modern audience.

In the following subchapters relating to performance practice, we will explore and analyze what were considered expressive goals for singers by composers and/or their contemporaries. Some of the effects they advocate may seem excessive for our comparatively emotionally repressed times; others will not. You should inform yourself of the composer's own artistic priorities as you would his notes and rhythms and consider the spirit behind those priorities. Once you are able to verbalize his priorities, you can then move on to how they were achieved in the composer's time and assess what would be viable today. The spirit of the music is always relevant, and it is up to you to transmit that spirit into the sensibility of today's audience. I would like to add that it is better to overdo than to be reticent: You are communicating emotions, and emotions are messy.

MUSIC BEFORE MOZART

Baroque performance practice is such a huge and complex subject, it has become a specialty all its own. Should you desire to make this repertoire an important part of your career, I would encourage you to apprentice yourself to a well-known specialist in the field for at least a few years. If you possess an appetite for scholarly minutiae and a deep love for this repertory, you can thrive in this niche. Due to the complexity and contentiousness among scholars pertaining to virtually every topic related to Baroque music, I can only supply you with a few general guidelines here. A good place to begin for more detailed information would be Martha Elliott's book, *So You Want to Sing Early Music.*[2]

Pitch is a perfect example of a topic that we generally take for granted, but this, too, has become a field of research all its own in recent times with special relevance to performance practice of music before Mozart. Though we assume that A=440 has always been the law of god, it was not established as the norm until 1926. As a rule of thumb, Baroque music is generally performed at A=415 (i.e., a semitone lower than notated), though French Baroque music is often performed at A=390 (i.e., down a full tone from notated), though exceptions are rife. For an exhaustive study of this topic, you can consult *A History of Performing Pitch: The Story of 'A'* by Bruce Haynes.[3] While it is rarely the singer's responsibility to know at what pitch a composition should be performed, you would be wise to contact whatever organization has hired you to sing this repertoire to ascertain at what pitch you should learn your music: Forewarned is forearmed! As you know, a whole step transposition can feel very different in your throat, especially for music of this period that tends to hover in the passaggio. In order to learn your music, you either need a solid background of keyboard harmony or an electronic keyboard with a transposing function.

I do not subscribe to the notion that this repertoire should only be sung by singers with small voices to balance the relatively small orchestral forces. Here, as in all repertoire, the priorities must be clarity of diction, clarity of emotional communication, and phrase direction. These are attributes that can be achieved by voices of all sizes. Admittedly, smaller voices can be heard to their advantage far better in this repertoire than in most heavily orchestrated repertoire of the nineteenth century.

We should distinguish between vocal compositions in recitative style and in aria style. The earlier Baroque style was predominated by secco recitative only occasionally punctuated by arias and ariosi. The composers of recitative style that are most performed today are Monteverdi in Italy and his follower Cavalli; and in France, Lully, Marc-Antoine Charpentier, and Rameau. To execute these effectively, the recitatives should be studied in the same manner as the recitative of later eras (see chapter 3: "Ornamentation and Recitative") with the proviso that in operas of this era, the rhythms must be performed as written (not as free speech) and with a steady pulse, although the tempo of each phrase (defined by the length of the thought, rather than of the sentence) does not need to relate to the tempo of the previous phrase. Indeed, each phrase must be in the tempo that best reflects the expression behind the text.

The most important treatise on contemporary performance practice from the Baroque era is Pier Francesco Tosi's *Opinioni d'cantori antichi e moderni* of 1723. It became widely disseminated in a German translation by Johann Friedrich Agricola in 1757.[4] The treatise is primarily a teaching manual aimed at the voice teacher. As such, it covers both what singers of the time were expected to be able to execute (including appoggiaturas, trills, ornaments, and cadenzas) and the methods by which those multifarious skills should be taught.

For example, ornaments in da capo arias were expected to be improvised during performance, which is nearly a lost art today. "Tosi cautions the singer against writing out the divisions [i.e., ornaments] in the [da capo] arias even as a pedagogical means to become more comfortable with the improvisations that he was expected to provide in the last two sections of the da capo aria, namely the B and A sections. Yet evidence from some eighteenth-century sources indicate that this was precisely what was done. Angus Heriot narrates an incident in which Caffarelli was incapable of performing in Naples because he had lost his written-out cadenzas."[5] Tosi then dedicates twenty pages to how those improvised divisions should be taught as well as the rules that they must follow.

Tempo rubato is generally considered to belong exclusively to performance practice of music of the nineteenth century. This is a misconception: "Tosi, like other discriminating musicians, considered the appropriate application of tempo rubato to be critical aspect of the singer's good taste and expressivity. . . . Tosi was one of the first writers to discuss tempo rubato, which he considered critical to good taste: 'Whoever does not know how to stretch out the notes [rubare il tempo] can certainly neither compose nor accompany himself and remains deprived of the best taste and finest insight.'"[6] Taste and expressivity are primary concerns of virtually every composer from every era, as you will see discussed in nearly every chapter dealing with performance practice.

The use or withholding of vibrato was seen as an expressive device in all Baroque vocal music, and vibrato was not expected to be an automatic default, as it is now. Singers of our time must find a healthy way to withhold their vibrato, which is much more challenging than it sounds.

Performers of French Baroque music will need to learn how to execute *notes inégales*, which is the precursor of the modern jazz "swing." Ornamentation of this repertoire is both different from, and more liberal than, that of Italian Baroque repertoire. The principal treatise on French Baroque ornamentation[7] pertains to keyboard ornaments rather than vocal ornaments, though you will undoubtedly be required to execute these instrumental ornaments vocally. There are additional vocal expressive devices particular to this repertoire that must be learned if you choose to specialize in this repertoire, in addition to a familiarity with historical pronunciation (whose use will vary from production to production). Grace and beauty were the performance ideals of the French Baroque,[8] and should be yours, too, when performing this repertoire.

As always, your priority must be communicating the spirit of the music. Nicolas Harnoncourt, one of the leading proponents of historically informed performances of Baroque music in the twentieth century, wrote: "Clearly, an interpretation that was historically uninformed but musically alive would be preferable [to 'those familiar musical performances which are often historically impeccable, but which lack all vitality.'] Musicology should never become an end in itself, but rather provide us with the means to make the best rendition, since a performance is only faithful to the original when a work is allowed to come most beautifully and most clearly to expression, something which happens only when knowledge and a sense of responsibility ally themselves with the deepest musical sensitivity."[9]

MOZART

For years I wondered on what basis critics anointed some singers as great Mozart stylists and others as not. While I recall no critic ever explaining or justifying his choices, I was also struck by the fact that there was a common agreement across the industry as to who belonged in which category. I embarked on a listening journey to ascertain what traits all the anointed great Mozart stylists shared.

The results confounded my expectations. First of all, neither the color nor the size of the instrument had any bearing on whether one was considered a Mozart stylist: Large, vibrato-laden voices were represented alongside slender, silvery ones. Rather, it is the way the singer used their instruments that admitted them into this elite society (or excluded them).

The first common trait of all of the Mozart stylists is an acute awareness of the direction of each phrase (see chapter 1: "Know Where You're Going"), which is generally the penultimate note of each phrase. If there was a high note within the phrase prior to the phrase's goal, it was treated as an attraction en route to the phrase's goal, rather than as a goal in itself. I do not mean to imply that the high notes were uniformly sung softly (though I remember an important New York voice teacher once confiding to me that soft high notes were commonly considered to be "morally superior" to loud high notes within the opera industry); rather, these high notes were treated as leading to the principal goal of the phrase. The exception to this rule is Mozart's unhinged characters who are unable to control themselves, such as Donna Elvira and Elettra.

The other common trait among the Mozart stylists, related to the concept of directionality, is the intentionality of their phrasing: They each give the impression that they have decided how each phrase should be sculpted, and they execute it precisely how they have decided.

These two traits, directionality and intentionality, and only these two traits defined who was admitted to the rarified club of Mozart stylists, and who was detained at the door.

There is a common conception that no portamenti are permitted in Mozart. I remember Elisabeth Schwarzkopf, one of the definitive Mozart stylists, reprimanding a young singer for committing this (in her words) "tasteless sin." This did not sit well with me, and I rushed home and listened to Schwarzkopf's seminal recording of Donna Elvira in *Don Giovanni*, where I discovered that her performance was rich in portamenti! Then I listened to many other examples of portamenti in Mozart singing, both among the anointed and among those singers celebrated for their performances of anything other than Mozart. My conclusion was that the wider the vibrato a voice possesses, the more the portamenti are magnified and the less they were tolerated. The slenderer voices often employed it with impunity and were never criticized for it. It is important to know your instrument and to know what works well for it.

THE *BEL CANTO* COMPOSERS

Without doubt, this is where the greatest disparity exists between how we *think* that this repertoire should be performed and how it actually *was* performed in the time of the composers, often under their direct supervision. We who have been raised in a time in which the highest ideal has been *come scritto*, i.e., performing exactly as notated and nothing more, have come to believe that music by these composers should be performed elegantly and dispassionately above all. I liken this to the equally erroneous perception that ancient Greek statuary was intended to communicate cool perfection. This perception has been based on the fact that nearly all the pieces that have survived are made of white marble. The truth, however, is that these statues were painted in their day, often gaudily, but the paint has worn off over time, leaving nothing but the naked marble. For centuries, art lovers have been basing their love of this statuary on a false premise,[10] and lovers of *bel canto* operas have been equally misled by their received wisdom.

The most important and influential treatise on vocal technique is *Ecole de García: traité complet de l'art du chant* by Manuel García fils,

Mayence, Paris: Schott 1847 (Teil 2), most recently translated by Francis Keeping (due for publication). Manuel Patricio Rodríguez García was the son of tenor Manuel del Pópulo Vicente Rodriguez García (also known as Manuel García the Senior), who created many roles for Rossini and other great composers of the period. Manuel Garcia Jr.'s books deal with much more than vocal technique: They are the best guides to interpretation of the *bel canto* repertoire that exist. In Garcia's treatise, I was shocked to learn that he advocated extreme emotionalism, based on the text and situation, to an extent that I have never encountered in anything other than the interpretation of Verismo repertoire. I will include a brief example from his book, in which he lays out how twenty-nine measures from the recitative preceding Assur's aria from *Semiramide* by Rossini should be (or might be) interpreted (see example a). Garcia begins by introducing the scene and aria thus, which I think important enough to quote in full:

> *Assur, devoured by ambition and pride, expresses implacable hatred and pursues the new king who, in elevating himself to the throne, has annihilated his power. He had already murdered the old king Nino with poison in the hope of seizing the scepter for himself; and now, meditates the assassination of the new king. When he is about to enter the tomb of the Assyrian monarch, he is surprised to see his victim, and is suddenly struck by a mysterious disturbance, his imagination presents him with terrible ghosts.*
>
> *The desire for revenge, anger, profound terror, delirium, the fear of death, and pleading prayer are all different dramatic colors that alternately paint this passionate scene. When different but slightly distinct feelings succeed one another, it is the duty of the pupil not only to characterize them, but also, to discriminate them and give each their space, or he will find that an overwhelming precipitation of elements only cause one effect to destroy the other and confuse the impressions of the listeners.*

If you turn to Garcia's annotations in Rossini's music, you will see that he has spelled out his interpretation of the subtext for each phrase, such as "with anger," "extremely menacing," and "with surprise," leading

excerpt from Rossini's *Semiramide*

ultimately to "delirious" and "beseechingly," and has included detailed vocal instructions on how to best achieve these effects, such as "suffocated voice, moved by emotion," and musical instructions serving the same goal.

I do not believe that Garcia is setting forth this example to show how this recitative must be interpreted; rather, he is showing how it might be interpreted effectively. He is establishing a methodology for analysis and interpretation that we can benefit from today. Garcia has scrupulously analyzed each line of the text in relation to the dramatic situation and has made decisions about the character and what he is feeling. He simultaneously gives suggestions on how those feelings are best achieved vocally.

Garcia is implicitly advocating that singers must bring a wider range of expressive devices to his singing of this music than I might have thought either possible or appropriately tasteful. Clearly my preconceptions, based on the received wisdom of my time, were wrong. The *bel canto* composers wanted this level of analysis and expression applied to their music: They wanted the marble and the paint. I would contend that this is what Rossini meant when he stated that a "mastery of style acquired both through training and through listening" was required to perform the music of his time effectively. Note that this requirement came last; it was preceded by the possession of a beautiful instrument and a fine technique. Stylistic mastery can only be achieved by discipline, but communication of the emotions that lie within the score is the ultimate goal of the singer.

Where does this leave the performers of today, in which the stylistic expectations of conductors and listeners are far different from those of the 1830s? Begin by making the same sort of dramatic and musical analyses as Garcia, but apply your conclusions judiciously and selectively. Nearly all of Garcia's expressive recommendations can be achieved within the sensibilities of our time, except the most extreme ones, such as overt sobs. Listen to Adelina Patti's recording of Bellini's "Ah! non credea" from *La Sonnambula*, in which she employed her exquisite instrument and technique in the service of creating a mood of ineffable sadness, which would undoubtedly be received enthusiastically by today's conductors and audiences. Use your judgment and execute your choices with total conviction!

It is important to remember that *bel canto* repertoire is a celebration of the singer's art and the possibilities of the classically trained voice. Its cornerstone is the two-part aria, described by Joseph Kerman thus: "The singer begins with a lyric aria, then changes his mind because of a message or something heard off-stage, then sings a vehement cabaletta to ring down the curtain."[11] This can only be viewed as an opportunity for the audience to become acquainted with the technical and artistic strengths and weaknesses of a singer. In these three to ten minutes, one can assess the singer's tone color, legato, ability to execute fioratura, and ability to transfix and move the public. When performing these arias, in order to be successful, you must seize the limelight and revel in the opportunity to strut your stuff.

VERDI AND WAGNER

According to the late opera historian and voice teacher Randy Mickelson, in the early decades of the nineteenth century, the tessitura of the *bel canto* roles crept higher. This resulted in more vocal excitement for the audiences. On the other hand, it made the words more difficult to understand, since a higher tessitura requires more vowel modification for vocal comfort than music with a lower tessitura.

Both Verdi and Wagner were aware of both the benefits and drawbacks that resulted from the higher tessitura. Both composers chose to assert the importance of the words over the excitement resulting from the higher tessitura, yet with different results.

Verdi was perhaps the greatest composer for the classically trained voice that the world has known. He understood its practical limitations and, over time, found solutions to vocal challenges that satisfied both the singers and their audiences.

I have taught opera composers, both aspiring and established, how to write for the voice. Knowing the profound impact that such instruction can have on the future of our art form, I have been highly circumspect with the examples I have chosen to guide my students. Inevitably, it has been Verdi to whom I have turned who provides the best paradigms for such essential topics as tessitura versus range (including which range to compose for each Fach in order to best impart essential textual information); what vowels to avoid on high notes and the passaggio; the differences between the Fachs, and how to best complement their natural capabilities in order to allow expression and communication.

Verdi lowered the tessitura for most vocal categories with the obvious result being that the words can be understood with a minimum of vowel modification. However, with a substantial part of a Verdi role now lying in a naturally less-resonant part of singers' ranges, the problem of projection became apparent, negating the benefits of enunciation of a lower tessitura. In order to fill the large theaters that Verdi's operas require (because of their large orchestral and choral forces), it became apparent that it was not the size of the singers' middle voice that determined their success in this repertoire, but its color. Those singers whose voices had a metallic edge that allowed them to cut through an orchestra had greater success in being heard than singers with larger, rounder voices devoid of this edge. The technical term for this vocal attribute is squillo, and contrary to what one might expect, it is the presence of squillo, particularly in the middle voice, that characterizes a voice as dramatic, rather than lyric. One need only hear a few middle voice notes sung by the great Verdi singers of the past, such as Rosa Ponselle, Zinka Milanov, and Renata Tebaldi, to recognize this quality. Generally, the lower a role's tessitura, the more dramatic it is considered to be, and the more squillo is essential to the singer's success.

If you are in any doubt as to whether your voice is dramatic or lyric, you must rely on the ears of your teacher and coach. Remember, it is not the sheer amplitude of the instrument that assigns it these labels, but its color. Counterintuitively, there exist large lyric voices (voices with great amplitude but lacking in squillo) and small dramatic voices (voices without great amplitude but with considerable squillo). Assuming that there is common agreement as to where your voice belongs, you can begin choosing the repertoire that would fit your instrument in the ears of those in the opera industry with the capability to help you move forward in your career. The Germans[12] have categorized virtually every standard opera role as being dramatic or lyric, and you would be wise to choose repertoire that narrowly subscribes to that category (Fach) until your career is well established. No matter how elegantly a lyric soprano sings an aria from *La forza del destino* or a dramatic soprano sings *La traviata*, their performances will be received with puzzlement, if not derision, by professionals.

Verdi is the composer that supposed opera cognoscenti and many opera enthusiasts most frequently cite as requiring only a great voice (presumably with squillo) and nothing else. It is worth exploring Verdi's own views on what he looked for in singers of his music.

In August 1846, when corresponding with impresario Alessandro Lanari about the casting of the title role of the first Macbeth, he wrote: "Varesi is the only singer in Italy who can play the role [Macbeth] I am thinking of, not only because of his singing, but also by virtue of his temperament and his appearance. All other, even those better than he, would be less suitable. I do not wish to say anything against Ferri, who is better looking, has a more beautiful voice, and is perhaps a better singer, but he would not play the role as well as Varesi." And twenty-five years later, he wrote to his publisher about the requirements of singing Amneris in Aida: "Voice alone, however beautiful (and that's difficult to judge in an empty room or theatre), is not enough for this role [Amneris]. So-called vocal finesse means little to me. I like to have roles sung the way I want them, but I can't provide the voice, the temperament, the 'je ne sais quoi' that one might call the spark. It's what is usually understood by the phrase, 'to be possessed by the devil.'"[13] And again in 1856 when corresponding about casting the role of Cordelia in a planned opera based on King Lear: "I know only three singers who could do it [Cordelia]. . . . All three have weak voices but great talent, spirit, and feeling for the stage."[14]

These quotes provide incontrovertible evidence that Verdi did not prize voice above all. On the contrary, "temperament" and "feeling for the stage" seem to be what he prized above all, which we might interpret as charisma today. This is an indefinable characteristic, but it something easily apprehensible to audiences and critics alike. Creating the character by any and all means was for him the ultimate goal of the singer. Furthermore, vocal coloration in the service of the character (and at the expense of beautiful vocalism) was something he not only condoned but encouraged, as he wrote to librettist Salvatore Cammargo: "And these numbers [duet between Lady Macbeth and her husband, and the Sleepwalking Scene] must definitely not be sung: they must be acted and declaimed in a voice hollow and veiled: otherwise the effect will be lost."[15]

Finally, when asked to preside over a commission on vocal training, Verdi wrote: "I should like the young student, who by now should have a strong knowledge of music and a well-trained voice, to sing, guided only by his own feelings. This will be singing, not of such-and-such a school, but of inspiration. The artist will be an individual. He will be himself, or, better still, he will be the character he has to represent in the opera."[16]

Clearly, possessing a dramatic voice was not of absolute importance to Verdi. He was looking for artistic communication, achieved both through theatrical and musical means. Finding the means of communication for yourself is the purpose of this volume.

Richard Wagner, like his contemporary Verdi, chose to address the incomprehensibility of the contemporary singers' delivery of the texts by lowering the tessitura of his operas. Wagner, who wrote his own libretti, was extremely interested in having his words understood and put a particularly high priority on getting the words across to the audience. To this end, he developed something that he called *Sprechtgesang* (song-speech or speech-song) as a compositional paradigm. *Sprechtgesang,* in its delivery, inhabits the land between aria and recitative, and as such, is most akin to what had been labeled *arioso.* Among his models for *Sprechtgesang* was the dialogue between Tamino and the Speaker in *Die Zauberflöte,* which requires from the singers a clarity of enunciation on one hand, balanced by legato and beautiful tone on the other. Unlike Italian recitative (and even Italian arioso), the note lengths in Wagner's *Sprechtgesang* are often extremely protracted far beyond normal speech, making intelligibility particularly challenging for the singer.

The challenge of being understood in Wagner is exacerbated by the relentless thickness of the orchestration. Unlike Verdi, who had full awareness of and sensitivity for the natural strengths and weaknesses of voices, Wagner does not exhibit commensurate consideration for, or understanding of, the human voice and its limitations. Both composers set important textual information in the lower-middle register, but when doing so, Verdi generally thinned out his orchestration so the words could be heard over the orchestra. Wagner did no such thing. This necessitated an even greater dependence on squillo to project both tone and words in the singers' weakest range than in Verdi's music.

This need for volume and the ability to cut through the orchestral texture in the singers' lower-middle range gave rise to entirely new vocal categories: the Heldensopran (i.e., heroic soprano), the Heldentenor, and the Heldenbariton, aka Wagnerian soprano, tenor, and baritone. This former moniker also takes into account the generally heroic aspects of the roles that Wagner assigned to these vocal categories. Whereas we often describe mezzo sopranos and basses as "Wagnerian" because of the volume and cut in their voices, they are never referred to as Heldenmezzosoprane [*sic*] or Heldenbässe [*sic*], presumably because the characters that Wagner assigned to these vocal categories rarely exhibit heroism.

Because of the great volume and cut required of the Wagnerian voices, the added thickness in the lower-middle voice frequently results in voices with reduced range on top. Wagner recognized this, and he composed many of his great roles that demand few high notes, like Siegmund and Parsifal for the tenors, and Sieglinde and Kundry for the sopranos.

Wagner's adoption of lower tessitura had additional philosophical meaning for him. He contended that German vocal cords were physiologically different from those of other nationalities and were inherently superior. He wrote that lower tessitura was a criterion of national identity: Germans spoke and sang with a lower tessitura not only because of their different (and superior) vocal cords, but because it reflected their natural essence: Germans were sincere and more connected to nature and their community than people from other nations. In contrast to the effete Italians and Frenchmen who spoke and sang in a higher tessitura, the Germans were solid and simple *Volk* who practiced superior, timeless, traditional values, rather than superficial constructs like high art, which was invented and practiced by the French and Italians. He contended that higher speech and singing was unnatural and antithetical to both the German voice and to the spirit of its people.[17] If one were to take Wagner at his word, only Germans would be suited to sing his music. Luckily, his xenophobic attitude toward singing never took hold, as evinced by the many great non-German singers who continue to excel in singing his music.

He was, unsurprisingly, firm in his conviction that German vocalism was superior to Italian vocalism for singing his music. He wrote to the vocal pedagogue Julius Hey in 1875, during preparations for the first Bayreuth Festival: "What good does it do me when, no matter how beautiful the notes I write, I can find no singer who understands how to sing them?"[18] In his letters, Wagner complained about the "the thoughtless adoption of Italian vocalism," though he paradoxically stipulated that the tonal beauty of the Italian school should not be sacrificed when singing his music, thereby tacitly conceding that the Italians did something well in the area of vocal training. Though we can never know what specific aspects of contemporary Italian vocalism Wagner did not like, we can speculate that the emotional vocal effects espoused by Garcia might have rubbed him the wrong way. In any case, those effects were not promulgated by those early Bayreuth singers who left us recordings. What we do know is that Wagner espoused a "German, or fatherland *bel canto*." He did not elucidate on what he meant by this, but he clearly wanted to appropriate certain aspects of Italian *bel canto* for German ownership.

It would be remiss of me to neglect to mention the prevailing performance practice in the generations immediately following Wagner's death, which gained the epithet of the "Bayreuth Bark." Under his widow's (mis) guidance, Wagner's interest in legato and tonal beauty was jettisoned in favor of an obsession with volume and projection of consonants at all costs. Those costs were all too often vocal misalignment, and ultimately, vocal damage. I reject the notion that Wagner would have condoned such a practice, for the simple reason that ugly sounds detract from the music that he composed.

What we do know is that Wagner's work with singers began with exhaustive reading rehearsals of the text. Presumably this was to consider the character through his/her text, much as is being advocated in this book, both by me and by others. In order to accomplish his dual goals of enunciation and legato, Wagner must have been searching for practitioners of a vocal technique characterized by freedom, with resonance and clarity of diction as its byproducts, rather than its goals.

VERISMO

Because the Verismo repertoire was composed much closer to our time, and the composers' favorite interpretations were recorded, it is much easier for us to draw conclusions about what is required when performing their music. Michael Scott, in his *The Record of Great Singing*,[19] writes "Boito and Ponchielli [put] the singer in the front line in direct combat with the orchestra, which inevitably led to a more vehement and dramatic vocal style. These developments culminated in the verismo school with its exaggerated and often unmusical pathos." Clearly Mr. Scott's musical tastes did not correspond with those of the composers themselves. He continues, "The effect of it all on Italian singing can be heard readily enough on any number of records made in the first two decades of this [twentieth] century; impure tone, obtrusive vibrato, crude attack and rough execution . . . ."

It would be useful for us to focus on what the composers themselves looked for in their singers, rather than Mr. Scott's disparaging assessment of them. When Mascagni had the opportunity to cast and conduct a truly authoritative recording of his opera *Cavalleria Rusticana* (financed by Mussolini), he chose soprano Lina Bruna Rasa, who had been languishing in a mental institution, to be his Santuzza and Beniamino Gigli to be his Turiddu. To say that Bruna Rasa's singing is emotionally charged is a vast understatement. She sings every phrase as if it were her last. Her voice is beautiful and powerful, but that is not what leaves a lasting impression; it is her vivid communication of the text and the emotion behind it that haunts you. As for Gigli, the most elegant of tenors, there is a story, probably apocryphal, that Mascagni asked the tenor to sing the Siciliana with wide open, spread vowels in his passaggio and above, like an untrained peasant boy. When Gigli explained that singing the aria in that manner would damage his voice, Mascagni apparently demurred. Whether true or not, that story, Gigli's singing of the entire role, and Bruna Rasa's singing strongly suggest that the communication of raw emotions, rather than elegant singing, were the composer's priority.

Another example would be Cilea's preferred interpreters for his opera *Adriana Lecouvreur*. Though premiered by another soprano, he wrote on numerous occasions that his favorite interpreter of the title role was Magda Olivero. Olivero brought a huge repertoire of special effects to her interpretations, which translate as hyper-emotional and affecting interpretations. I would strongly recommend that every singer listen to a recording of Olivero's 1969 San Jacopino (Firenze) concert to hear her stunning performances of Italian arias. I sent a soprano student of mine to work with Olivero in 2012, when Olivero was 102 years old, in order to gain insight into her artistic process. To our mutual surprise, Olivero's seemingly spontaneous special effects were anything but: they were calculated in excruciating detail. A typical instruction was to begin the note (marked forte) at mezzo piano for one beat, crescendo for 1.5 beats to forte, hold it there for another 1.5 beats, then diminuendo to piano for 1 beat, hold that volume for another beat, then portamento to the next note.

Olivero would articulate the emotional effect she was aiming to communicate, and the best musical means she had discovered to accomplish it. (Stories abound of Callas's equally calculated and meticulous strategies for achieving her musical effects.) This is not to say that every singer needs to plan the details of every musical effect she desires to achieve, but without being able to articulate the emotion you are trying to convey, you have no hope of conveying it. Recordings exist of Enrico Caruso and Giuseppe de Luca singing selections from *Adriana Lecouvreur* with the composer at the piano. Like Olivero's interpretations, they strike one as extrovertly emotional by their use of special effects, such as those listed above.

I would strongly encourage anyone who loves this repertoire to become acquainted with two other great paragons of Verismo interpretation: Claudia Muzio and Franco Corelli.

MODERN MUSIC

A great percentage of my career has involved performing music of our time. Rather than devoting a separate chapter to contemporary music, I have come to conclude that all of its issues for performers are the same as for all music since 1900, but in differing proportions.

In general, works of the twentieth and twenty-first centuries can be classified as those for which the musical gesture and the spirit of the music is of greater importance than the letter of the music, and those for which the reverse is true.

The primary vocal composers of the Second Viennese School: Schoenberg and Berg, confront us with a set of challenges new to its time. In particular, they employed what they called Sprechgesang (speech-song) or Sprechstimme (speech-voice) in their Expressionist phase (i.e., prior to 1921), in which the general contours of the phrase are notated, but the exact pitches are meant to be approximated. In the foreword to *Pierrot Lunaire* (1912), Schoenberg explained how his Sprechstimme should be executed: The indicated rhythms should be adhered to, but unlike in ordinary singing where a constant pitch is maintained throughout a note, here the singer "immediately abandons it by falling or rising. The goal is certainly not at all a realistic, natural speech." Nor is the goal anything that resembles singing: rather the general effect is that of hyper-emotional speech. Here there is no question that the musical gesture is everything, since exact pitches are ruthlessly to be avoided. Communication of the expressive content is the highest priority in Expressionist repertoire.

After Schoenberg's and Berg's adoption of serialism in 1921, this priority changed dramatically. From that time on, the letter of the music became the priority for them. Lucy Shelton, perhaps the foremost interpreter of vocal music of this repertoire and of music of the late twentieth century, told me that in complex repertoire such as this, "The character is all in the music . . . it is shown it all the details of tempi, range, rhythms, articulations, dynamics, and obviously the text." When I inquired about the expressive content of Gesture in this music, she responded: "I pay attention to everything on the page. I do not need to analyze the gestures: I just do them." In other words, interpretation is irrelevant and unnecessary in this repertoire.

Clearly this is a sea change from vocal music from earlier centuries, in which the singer must commit to an interpretation in order to communicate effectively. While in modern music the question of musical priorities is sometimes a black-or-white question, some modern music lies in the gray area between, with one passage requiring exactitude and the next seeming to be more about the gesture. If you are singing the music with a living composer, you will have the luxury of consulting the source and perhaps negotiating with him or her. (Please see my interview with Davóne Tines for more light on this subject.) If the composer lived in the era of recordings, analyze recordings of the composer's favorite interpreters to glean what their priorities and intentions might have been, and extrapolate from those conclusions as your guide.

A huge skill set can be required in learning modern music. Know your limitations. Shelton said: "One most know one's strengths and weaknesses. I start by learning the pitches, because rhythms come much more easily to me." Though perfect pitch is a plus, it is not a necessity. Try to look at score before accepting the gig. Remember that not all offers equal good opportunities: It is wiser to decline an offer than to not succeed in a challenge you have unwisely undertaken. As a rule of thumb, I would recommend that you give yourself 50 percent more time than you anticipate you will need to learn any non-tonal score. My experience has proven that most people underestimate the difficulty of a challenge and overestimate their abilities. You must also know your sensibilities as well as your capabilities: "To sing this repertoire, you must thrive on challenges. The harder the music is, the more excited I have always been," concluded Shelton. Know whether you are, or are not, someone who thrives on unraveling complex musical details. You do not have to excel in everything: You will enjoy your greatest successes in the repertoire that suits you both vocally and temperamentally.

5

Song Interpretation

The most successful song performances are those that are approached as miniature dramas, and with the same level of scrutiny and inquiry as opera roles. Since songs are given to you without a context, it is up to you to provide one for yourself. When learning a new song, begin by studying the text and asking yourself if the singer/protagonist is singing to someone else or to himself. If it is to someone else, to whom? It is particularly important to consider what has occurred that compels the singer/protagonist to express the text. Be sure to consider where each new thought begins and ends for the character, just as you would for your opera arias. Your job is to take the listener on a journey: not some vague journey, but the character's emotional journey as indicated in the text and the music. Consider the mood you are trying to communicate and whether it changes through the course of the song.

In song repertoire, because you are nearly always responsible for inventing a context that supports the text and the music, you have far more creative input than in opera. In song repertoire, you have an opportunity to collaborate intimately with the composer, and you should embrace that opportunity. Please read my sample analysis of Schumann's Du bist wie eine Blume in chapter 13 as a paradigm for how to approach song interpretation.

Your goal must be to create the character and scene with your voice, keeping physical gestures to a minimum. The more you gesture, the greater the likelihood that your performance will be deemed to be unstylistic and inappropriate. In song repertoire, gesturing distracts from your communication, rather than supports it. Many famous opera singers feel stifled by singing recital repertoire for this reason, while others feel liberated by it. While I have not focused on this aspect of song interpretation in my chapters on performance practice of *Lieder* and *Mélodie*, scarcity of gesture is one of the principal distinguishing traits of song performance versus opera performance and is of vital importance to how your performance is received.

More acutely than in opera, in song repertoire you must consider the role of the accompaniment, because in most circumstances you will share the stage only with a pianist. Does the accompaniment play a role beyond merely supporting what you are expressing? If so, what is that role, and does it change through the course of the song? The accompaniment often represents something concrete, like rain or the movement of a body of water. Alternately, it can suggest a general emotional state. It is your job to discuss with the pianist what the function of the accompaniment is at all times in order to make sure that you are in complete agreement. Both you and your pianist will find these discussions inspiring and artistically empowering, and they are sure to help you function as one artistic unit.

Discussions relating to the role of the accompaniment can become more complex (and even more interesting) in songs where the composer has included one or more instruments in addition to, or instead of, the piano. In Schubert's *Auf dem Strom*, for example, the French horn may sometimes represent the beloved, at other times it may represent a storm, and at other times it may represent nostalgia for a home that will never be seen again. The piano sometimes echoes these representations and may sometimes represent other things (like the current of the river or the tears of the protagonist), and sometimes it supports the emotional world of the voice and of the horn. Discussions with your musical partners will be fruitful for all of you, and I encourage you to initiate them. Remember that there is no correct interpretation beyond whatever resonates best with you.

Since chamber music is about collaboration, there will be no one assumed leader for these discussions in your rehearsals. Therefore, you should arrive with the relevant questions about the music thoroughly considered and ready to articulate, and you should be prepared to discuss with your musical partners whatever conclusions you have made on your own. It is possible that the instrumentalist(s) are unaccustomed to such discussions and have never considered a text. Once they understand the goal of these discussions, they are likely to embrace them enthusiastically. You should supply them with copies of the text and translations at least a week in advance of your first scheduled rehearsal together as a sign of respect for their time. Approach these and all rehearsals with an open mind and a spirit of inquiry, and your entire team will grow together and enjoy the process. If everyone on your team shares the specific goals of communication, the music and your audience will reap the benefits of your labor.

GERMAN *LIEDER*

From the beginning of recorded music (and probably extending back to the period of composition) until the 1950s, *Lieder* was sung by beautiful voices communicating the spirit of the poems they sang. This was often achieved through many vocal expressive devices, including fluctuations of tempo, bending of rhythms, and liberal portamenti between notes. Some protean examples worth your attention are the great Danish tenor Helge Rosvaenge singing Strauss's *Freundlich Vision* in 1936, in which the mood is so ravishingly projected that all details become irrelevant; and Marcella Sembrich's 1913 recording of Schubert's *Wohin?*, and Elisabeth Schumann's 1932 recording of Schubert's *Das Lied im Grünen*, which are performed with the sort of rhythmic freedom we tend to associate with Luciano Pavarotti or Giuseppe di Stefano singing Neapolitan songs, in which rhythmic alignment between melody and accompaniment is of secondary importance to communicative spontaneity.

This freedom to express the spirit of the text and the music over the letter of the music was not the exception among the great artists of the period, but the rule. One need only listen to the *Lieder* recordings of Lotte Lehmann and the many recordings of Strauss *Lieder* with the composer at the piano for clear evidence of the artistic priorities of the age. Brahms, when coaching an early interpreter of his *Vier Ernste Gesänge* who was unable to execute the final diminuendo marked in the score, instructed him instead to crescendo to an fff instead of the marked piano. Scores were not seen as holy writ to be followed slavishly, but as a means of communication.

As a young student in London, I had the honor to accompany many *Lieder* coachings given by the great German baritone Gerhard Hüsch, who himself had coached with Brahms's disciples. Thus was I able to learn the great *Lieder* traditions from a brilliant singer who could trace his artistic lineage back to the great composers. One day I was accompanying Brahms's *Feldeinsamkeit*. When we arrived at the phrase "*mir ist, also ob ich längst gestorben bin*" (I feel as if I have long been dead), Hüsch indicated that the phrase should be performed at half tempo, reflecting the spirit of the text and the corresponding harmonic ambiguity of the phrase. I, being a callow youth, challenged him, asking why Brahms had not indicated half tempo if that was what he had wanted. Hüsch's reply was simply, "He expected musicians to be musical."

The evolution of *Lieder* performance in first half of the twentieth century can be characterized by a move from joyful freedom and spontaneity to joyless suppression and musical enslavement; from mood painting and storytelling to tics and mannerisms. Beginning in the 1950s, Elisabeth Schwarzkopf, relentlessly coached by her husband, record producer Walter Legge, ruthlessly expunged all spontaneity from *Lieder*, and replaced it with a slavish diligence to the letter of the score, with the addition of hyper-coloration of individual words at the expense of the gesture and storytelling. The net result was a focus on the local interpretation that overwhelmed the global. The Schwarkopf-Legge team changed the course of (some might say hijacked) *Lieder* interpretation in the mid-twentieth century, and their influence can still be felt to this day. Singers of other nationalities, like Gerard Souzay and Elly Ameling, followed their lead in non-German repertoire, but with less effect.

This evolution drew attention away from the composer and to the singer. Disingenuously representing herself as the humble servant and defender of the sacred art and the composer, she actually took the focus from the composer and relentlessly moved it to the interpreter, i.e., herself.

Recordings from the 1940s of Sophie's "Presentation of the Rose" from *Der Rosenkavalier* and the "Sandman's Song" from *Hansel and Gretel* show Schwarzkopf possessing a sunny, silvery instrument. Her inherent vocal quality would be considered that of a soubrette, better suited to characters like Susanna and Despina than to Countess Almaviva and Fiordiligi, roles for which she became identified. The seeds of her later artistic mannerisms can already be heard in her 1946 recording of Schubert's *Seligkeit*, in which she, unlike virtually every other interpreter, downplays the text's innocent joy and instead surprisingly transforms the song into an introverted expression of religious sublimity.

Beginning in the 1950s, all spontaneity and vulnerability has disappeared from her singing. Schubert's *Das Lied im Grünen*, so infectiously ebullient when sung by Elisabeth Schumann, is joyless and arch in Schwarkopf's 1952 recording accompanied by Edwin Fischer. Her 1974 recording of Schumann's *Liederkreis* is more about the performer than the songs. In her final 1981 recital recording with Geoffrey Parsons, Wolf's *Fussreise* fussily presents a simulacrum of the joy experienced during a walk in the country, rather than communicating the joy of the stroll itself. Her interpretation is so mannered and didactic it seems that she is explaining the joy to someone who has always been denied this experience. In these late recordings, the text and music are manipulated and tortured, communicating nothing beyond self-indulgence and self-aggrandizement.

There is a particular genius in Schwarzkopf's continual textual colorations, but in her later recordings, the effect is rather kaleidoscopic and blinding. Only upon later consideration does one realize that its way is Schwarzkopf's, and not that of the composers whom she claimed to revere.

In a 1980 interview, Schwarzkopf said: "... What my husband and I wanted is not just singing lines and phrases and words and pronunciation and the right tempo and the right useful color of that beautiful voice: no. We wanted really to convey the poetry by more than that, by the appropriate color. ..." In sentiments not unlike those voiced by Maria Callas (see the chapter 12: "Maria Callas: Self-Effacing Purist"), she continued, "We have to set our imagination to work when we sing *Lieder* ... we have the poem and the music and we try and study it as carefully as we can and find out from the way it has been composed—why the composer composed it just that way—and then we try and find the reason behind it and the emotional reason, and the situation, and the psychological reasons behind it; and try and give it the color of that particular emotion." Unlike Callas, Schwarzkopf did not practice what she preached. Rather than conveying the emotional color of the phrase or of the song, Schwarzkopf worked to convey the emotional color of individual words, divorced from their context. More honestly explaining her methodology and goals, she continued, "Sometimes you have to produce a new sounding voice, you have to have a very rich palette of colors, even that one voice you have only got but you still have to try and get so many colors as you possibly can, as you would have in life."

In sum, I would argue that Schwarzkopf's truth-seeking was taken to extreme conclusions, like some Talmudic scholars and followers of Fundamentalist religions. Her artistic interventions eventually obliterated the essence of the music and the text by losing sight of the big picture and the emotional message of the *Lieder*.

That said, I strongly applaud her spirit of inquiry: "[one must ask oneself] What's the psychological reason behind the way a crescendo is done, why [is a] crescendo, a decrescendo or a subito piano [indicated]? I just want . . . to feel the human reason behind the written-down things." I hope that you will commence your own search for musical and artistic truths, yet directed toward more humble goals.

FRENCH *MÉLODIES*

Since the bulk of this repertoire was composed in the twentieth century, after the beginning of recorded sound, assessing performance practice is a far simpler undertaking than with *Lieder*. If you consider that Poulenc was composing songs until 1960, you realize that French *Mélodie* is a relatively young genre.

Pierre Bernac (1899–1979) was the most influential interpreter and advocate of French *Mélodie* in the twentieth century. As a singer, he recorded much of the literature; he was the muse of Francis Poulenc, and premiered many his songs; wrote guides to interpretation of French song; and coached generations of singers in this repertoire. We should begin with his advice to singers regarding the challenge of interpretation: "The performance and interpretation of vocal music raise problems of a particular kind: two elements—a musical text and a literary text—must be analyzed and then synthesized. Obviously the literary text deserves the same care, the same scrupulous accuracy, in short the same respect that is demanded by the musical text. . . . When a composer sets a literary text to music, he has his personal conception of the feelings expressed in the text, and it is this feeling that he attempts to express in the music."[1] In other words, it is the singer's responsibility to analyze the possible interpretations inherent in the text and to commit to whatever interpretation the composer chose to accentuate, rather than one that may be interesting but conflicts with the music. When more than one interpretation can be inferred, you should choose whichever rings most true.

Listening to Bernac's recordings, they can be characterized by communication of the spirit of the music and the text in much the same way as *Lieder* was performed prior to 1950: with a freedom, sincerity, and spontaneity, and a low value placed on exact rhythmic alignment between voice and accompaniment.

Sadly, I never met Bernac. I did, however, have the opportunity to work with Bernac's contemporary, the great Swiss interpreter of French *Mélodie*, Hugues Cuenod (1902–2010). Cuenod possessed an irrepressible charm, a twinkle in his eye, and a sense of joyfulness that carried into his music-making. Even though I knew him in the 1980s, his musical sensibilities were those of an earlier time. He was a supportive and gentle mentor, who always taught with kindness. The only occasion that I can recall him becoming impatient was when a singer persisted in singing Duparc's *L'invitation au voyage* in a strict six beats per measure, rather than the two beats per measure that he insisted on. The latter allowed the singer more freedom to express the sentiments of the text on top of the musical depiction of the gentle rocking of the boat. Cuenod felt that performing the opening of the song in six drained the spirit from the music while drawing attention to the far less-important letter of the music.

It is enlightening to listen to Bernac's 1945 recording of this song (with Poulenc at the piano) and Charles Panzera's 1932 recording of the same song. Both of these artists perform the song in six beats per bar (as frowned upon by Cuenod), but neither is straitjacketed by this rigor: Both manage to seduce by vividly describing the land of sensuality by weaving around the beats, rather than slavishly adhering to them. They evoke a land of *luxe, calme, et volupté* unfettered by rules, whether rhythmic or moral. Bernac says, much like Magda Olivero (see chapter 4 on

Verismo performance practice): "All this of course is carefully thought out in advance, carefully calculated, worked at, clarified and perfected, and ... finally surrendered to the improvisation of the moment."[2] I do not believe that calculating every effect is the only way to achieve your artistic objectives, but I am convinced that you must know exactly what you are trying to communicate in order to succeed in doing so.

For a key to the performance practice of an even earlier time, listen to recordings of this repertoire sung by Maggie Teyte. Teyte was Debussy's favorite interpreter of the role of Mélisande, and having been coached thoroughly by him, she could be considered the ultimate authority on how to interpret his music. Listening to her recording of the *Chansons de Bilitis*, her interpretive freedom is immediately evident. Teyte here expresses the text in a parlando in which the words follow their natural rhythm as expressed by the character, rather than metronomically. Once you become acquainted with her art, you will be hooked into hearing more and more. Her interpretive priorities remain the same from song to song and composer to composer: communication of the spirit of the text as expressed by the music. In her own words: "Interpretation is the ultimate aim of the French school of singing. A beautiful but cold voice will win laurels in other lands, but the French will applaud a less beautiful voice if there is good interpretation behind it. There are so many tints— '*nuances*' they would call them—in the French language, demanding skillful production of the voice to offset the characteristics of modern French speech which do not make for attractive singing tone."[3]

Where *Lieder* leads, art songs of other nations follows. With the ascent of Elisabeth Schwarzkopf as the arbiter of *Lieder* interpretation, the priorities she exemplified carried into interpretation of *Mélodies*. Comparing Bernac's 1945 recording of Gounod's *Sérénade* with Gerard Souzay's recording a mere eighteen years later, it is easy to hear that a joyful expression of the spirit of the text and music has been replaced by a rigid adherence to the letter of the text and the music.

Both extremes can be heard on the concert stage today. By now, it should be clear where my artistic preferences lie.

6

Abstract Music and Vocalizes

This chapter considers how to construct an interpretation of vocal music that lacks a text. Most text-free vocal works that you will encounter are song-length vocalizes, though there are occasional operatic roles that fall into that category, like the role of Madeline in Philip Glass's *The Fall of the House of Usher*. The process for constructing these interpretations can also serve as a starting point for instrumentalists and conductors when approaching any abstract musical composition, i.e., any music without a stated narrative or a text.

Virtually all musical compositions composed between the Baroque era and the mid-twentieth century are based on contrast. All such music carries within it an implied drama: Will the contrasting elements be resolved? How and when will this occur?

It is the contrasting elements that define a work's musical form, and with it, its implied drama; and it is up to you to unlock and communicate that drama. Historically, the most significant contrast is tonal, and perhaps the easiest to identify. With any departure from the tonic key—which is certain to occur in any composition longer than a few seconds—there is a built-in harmonic tension that continues until the return to the tonic. As a performer, you can manipulate the tension to optimal effect only if you are aware of this tension and its concomitant drama.

The most common large-scale organizing musical principle based on tonality is sonata. Sonata can be thought of as a theatrical form of tonal contrast, initialized by tonal/dramatic contrast, leading to dramatic conflict (development), and concluded with conflict resolution. As such, it is a mini-drama whose contrasts can be characterized for maximum audience impact. Nearly all music of the eighteenth century is based on the Sonata principle, including nearly every aria by Mozart, Haydn, and Gluck. These composers maximized that dramatic potential of the form by aligning the contrasting tonalities with comparable emotionally contrasting texts. Basing your interpretation of this music on the texts as they relate to the music, as explored throughout this book, will result in rich, nuanced interpretations. On the rare occasion when you might encounter a wordless sonata form, such as Reinhold Gliere's Concerto for Coloratura Soprano, it is the drama of the form that must guide your interpretation, much as it guides instrumentalists and conductors in constructing their interpretations of sonatas, symphonies, and concertos.

Without the text to guide you, the music itself must become your guide. Listen to it analytically and imaginatively, and let it suggest to you the appropriate moods to communicate.

That said, you must shape the phrases here as elsewhere. Within a phrase, text-free music does not necessarily move to the same goal points as does music with text. In the latter, where the line is directed toward its ultimate or penultimate syllable in order to hold the audience's interest, the lines in vocalizes generally move to the point of greatest harmonic tension, which then resolves. Whether you have a strong background in music theory or not, you can apprehend these points of harmonic tension by listening for them. By approaching the music as an exploration of its emotional content, you are developing your own map of its moods and architecture, as discussed in chapter 1, "Know Where You're Going."

In addition to tonality, other musical elements that composers routinely contrast are dynamics, phrase lengths, texture, and color. An awareness of these contrasts can shape your interpretations, much as an awareness of a work's tonal contrasts.

It should be noted that there exists modern music and some early music that is not based on contrast, but on slowly unfolding, subtle, imperceptible changes. Perhaps at some point the listener realizes that the music has changed, but cannot track the changes, which is akin to looking in the mirror and being shocked that you no longer resemble your younger self, without being able to chart how it happened. Wide-ranging examples of this aesthetic are Luciano Berio's Sequenza III and much of

Morton Feldman's Three Voices; and it can be found in much music of Perotin, John Cage's Aria (in which the text is irrelevant), and the late Gabriel Fauré. The tools you have acquired in this book are irrelevant in this music, and you would be better off directing your interpretive energies elsewhere. Here you should sing what's on the page as accurately as possible and not bother with anything beyond that.

7

Conclusion

Performance Practice

I like to think that all operas exist somewhere on a continuum of artistic priorities, with one extreme being vocal elegance and purity, and the other extreme being technique-be-damned extreme emotionalism. I find it useful to place opera composers on the continuum, though any opera within a composer's oeuvre may lie to one side or the other of the composer's typical opera. Indeed, an aria or ensemble within an opera may carry a different priority than the remainder of the opera. Where a given composer, opera, or aria sits on the continuum is totally subjective; but identifying for yourself the priorities of whatever you are studying is a very fruitful activity, because you then can only achieve your artistic goals by first articulating them for yourself.

VOCAL ELEGANCE AND PURITY

I would characterize this side of the continuum by some of the tenets of *bel canto*, i.e., beautiful singing. Among those attributes, Rossini himself characterized these attributes as a beautiful instrument, even in tone from the bottom to the top of a singer's range; a beautiful sound on every note, regardless of pitch or vowel; and effortless vocal agility characterized by clarity of scales, arpeggios, trills, and staccatti. To this he also added a mastery of style acquired both through training and through listening.

TECHNIQUE-BE-DAMNED HYPER-EMOTIONALISM

This side of the continuum might be characterized by a goal of communicating emotion by the use of special effects, which may be totally incompatible with vocal elegance and purity. A small sample of these might be sobs; glottal attacks; gulps; audible intake or exhalation of breath; doubling, tripling, and quadrupling of selected consonants; manipulation of vibrato; manipulation of intonation (aka "blue notes"); accentuated slides between notes (aka "scooping"); and coloration of specific vowels contrary to healthy vocalism. Applied judiciously and thoughtfully, these special effects are all important elements of a singer's expressive vocabulary.

When I began writing this book, I contended that Mozart and the *bel canto* composers (Rossini, Donizetti, and Bellini) occupy the former end of the continuum, with the Verismo composers (including Puccini) occupying the latter extreme. My subsequent research, which can be found in chapter 4 under the subheading "The *bel canto* composers," has required me to rethink this contention.

My rough chart of the continuum of artistic priorities of opera composers would then look something like this:

Vocal elegance and purity	Technique-be-damned hyper-emotionalism
Mozart and Handel	
Verdi	
Most contemporary composers	
	Bel canto composers
	Verismo
	Expressionist music

PORTAMENTI AS AN EXPRESSIVE DEVICE

Portamenti, or the sliding between two notes, has been a contentious topic among singers, conductors, and coaches for the last century or more. A number of famous singers, such as Elisabeth Schwarzkopf and Elly Ameling, deemed all portamenti to be strictly forbidden stylistically in Mozart and in song repertoire, while practicing it extensively themselves!

My conclusions on this topic may provide a useful starting point as to what may be judged tasteful by musicians and audiences of today.

First of all, large, vibrato-laden voices must be much more judicious in their use of portamenti than leaner voices, simply because their instruments magnify this expressive device, often to the extent of spotlighting it to the exclusion of everything else. As an example of this, listen to any recording of Renata Tebaldi singing Mozart. It is easy to dismiss these recordings as a great artist ill-advisedly singing repertoire unsuitable to her voice and temperament. I would argue, however, that it is not her instrument that gives this impression, but the way she uses it. By her frequent sliding between notes both upward and downward, and by the high notes being the goal of her phrases, she is applying essential performance practice for Verismo repertoire to Mozart, and the results are quite perverse. In addition, her inclusion of "h's" in virtually all melismas gives an overall impression of flippancy that is ill-suited to the dramatic situations.

Obviously, portamenti can happen in two directions, upward and downward, and they can additionally be categorized by their speed of execution. The upward slide to the high note, especially when executed slowly, is generally referred to as "scooping," and is always described pejoratively. The impression that scooping leaves is that the high notes are very difficult for the singer to reach and can only be attained through the application of great effort, momentum, and perhaps prayer. This is an impression inimical to virtually all vocal repertoire and should be avoided. A quick slide between a lower note and a higher one can be extremely effective and can give the impression of enormous enthusiasm or, when accompanied by a diminuendo, of an inverted sigh. This can be a potent emotional device if one is cognizant of the danger of it being perceived as scooping if executed too slowly.

The portamento from a higher note to a lower one only carries an interpretive danger when departing from a very high note. You want to avoid giving the impression that you are eager to descend from a high note because it is uncomfortable or effortful. A downward portamento executed quickly and accompanied by a diminuendo can be the musical illustration of a sigh, which can be extremely effective when appropriate to the character and the situation, regardless of the era of the composition. Executed more slowly and without a diminuendo, the effect is one of extreme, uncontrollable emotionality and must be judged in relation to the character, the situation, and the era in which the work was composed.

III

MUSICAL MUSINGS

Some Vexing Musical Examples

In the course of your career, you are certain to encounter arias that make no sense to you, no matter how you approach them.

For years, Servilia's aria "S'altro che lagrime" from Mozart's *La clemenza di Tito* made no sense to me. Her text expresses vexation or perhaps anger at Vitellia for doing nothing to save her brother's life, even though she is in a position to easily do so. There is no other way to interpret the text. Yet Mozart set the text to an elegant Minuet in A Major. The music's mood is gentle, and it resists any attempt to render it fiery or agitated. I spent years puzzling over this opposition between text and music, and it greatly disturbed me, because I sensed I was overlooking something that would provide the key to my understanding. When I was preparing to conduct the entire opera, I was able to put the aria in context by observing it with a wider lens, and it suddenly struck me: Servilia, while expressing vexatious or even angry sentiments, is trying not to offend Vitellia, nor seem too argumentative, knowing that Vitellia is combustible and dangerous, and Servilia's hectoring could backfire. In spite of the text, Servillia is adopting a placating, nonthreatening tone in order to get Vitellia to do the right thing.

Another aria, Leonora's opening aria, "Tacea la notte placida," from *Il trovatore* gave me even more trouble. Leonora is recounting her undiluted joy at her first introduction to Manrico, the love of her life. Verdi chose to set this ecstatic cavatina in the key of A flat minor, which is about as dour a key as you can find. While I could invent many possibilities why Leonora might relate this jubilant story in a key that contradicts the text's sentiments, none of them felt true to me: Leonora is not a complicated character emotionally, and she would not speak with even a trace of irony or hidden conflict. After decades of feeling dense for not being able to come up with an explanation that I would buy for the conflict between the text and Verdi's setting of it, I decided that the time was overdue for me to enlist the help of my colleagues to come up with a plausible explanation. I thought that this would be the perfect opportunity to appeal to the hive mind of the internet by posting my conundrum on social media. Over a dozen singers, conductors, stage directors, and opera enthusiasts responded to my query within minutes. While most of the responses were explanations I had already considered and jettisoned, James Jordan, the founder of the opera blog Parterre Box, came up with a response that rang true to me. His detailed analysis demonstrated how the text, line by line, invited a modulation to the parallel major (i.e., A flat major). The arrival to the new key is perceived by us as particularly momentous and cathartic specifically because of its previous key. Jordan also posited that Verdi's audience would have perceived minor keys as unstable and requiring a resolution to major. I have no idea whether this latter assertion is accurate, but his explanation of the first key as a setup to the eventual arrival of the indisputably joyful key of A flat major makes perfect sense to me. I was immediately able to recall of a number of other instances from this period in Verdi's output where he utilized this same progression from minor to the parallel major, and each time the major was accompanied by a strong sense of emotional arrival.

My present conundrum is why Edgardo's aria "Fra poco a me ricovero" from Donizetti's *Lucia di Lammermoor*, which immediately precedes his suicide, is set in sunny D major. I suspect that I will soon give up and open the question to discussion on social media with my colleagues. This option is one of the advantages of living our modern age. In an earlier time, we would have had to simply perform those arias we hadn't made peace with, whether we could fake conviction or not.

When you encounter arias that stump you like those examples cited above, I recommend that you actively puzzle over them, looking at the text from every possible vantage point, and if none of your potential interpretations works with the music, then try to manipulate the mood of the music to correspond to your characterization. If none of this bears fruit artistically, there's no shame in eliciting the aid of superior minds, or at least other ones.

The (In)validity of Tradition in Vocal Music

The significance of tradition in interpretations of vocal music is a highly divisive issue. On the one hand, Mahler was said to have remarked, "Tradition is the memory of the last bad performance." One the other hand, John Fleming, a noted music critic, asserts that "tradition is the heart of classical music."

It would be wise to explore the types of traditions that we encounter in vocal music today (particularly opera) and to speculate about the reasons why they developed. From there we can assess their relevance and validity in our time.

The first category of traditions in vocal music is changes to the vocal line, such as changes in the text, syllabification, or word placement.

The second category is cuts. These cuts may shorten the playing time of the opera or give a singer less to sing. They might involve excising measures or pages of the score, or simply cutting the voice part while the accompanying continues as written.

A third category would be the interpolation of high notes, or the lengthening of high notes. An example of the lengthening of a high note occurs in Richard Strauss's own recording of his *Lied* "Zueignung," in which he accompanies Anton Dermota on the piano, as well as in the orchestral transcription. Here the climactic note that occurs on the word "Heilig" is held for two beats rather than the notated single beat, resulting in a measure of five beats, rather than four elsewhere. The interpolation of high notes often occurs in conjunction with the second category, i.e., letting the singer remain silent for some time while the accompaniment continues prior to an interpolated high note. There are hundreds of examples of this category of tradition, primarily in music of the *bel canto* repertoire, though it occasionally occurs later as well (the end of Violetta's aria "Sempre libera," or Manrico's "Di quella pira," for example).

A fourth category would be transpositions, either of single passages or of full arias.

We can conjecture as to why each of these categories of traditions arose. In each case, the reasons are quite obvious and require little guesswork.

The first category probably developed to make it easier for the audience to understand the words or for the singer to sing them, or both. For example, there are many instances in the role of Gilda in Verdi's *Rigoletto* and the role of Leonora in Verdi's *Il trovatore* where this occurs. We do not know whether Verdi sanctioned these changes, but they occur in performances of the earliest existing recordings of these operas and they probably originated much earlier. It should be noted that in his later operas, Verdi routinely avoided placing consonants and consonant clusters before high notes as he did here.

Very occasionally, a small cut is made in a score to facilitate performance, such as the frequent 14-measure cut in the second act quintet of *Un ballo in maschera*, because the syncopations Verdi indicated have tripped up many otherwise-brilliant sopranos, and a frequent 8-measure cut in the second act trio that poses grave intonation challenges. Puccini sanctioned a 15-measure cut in the second act duet of *La fanciulla del West*, ostensibly at the request of Enrico Caruso, which has now become standard practice in spite of the uncut version holding significant musical riches. Wagner grudgingly made cuts in many of his operas, at the vehement behest of his singers, who insisted they needed a rest.

Regarding the tradition of interpolating high notes, I cannot think of a single example in which a composer approved of this practice, particularly when it involves leaving out some of the preceding vocal line in order to rest for the interpolated held high note. As a young coach, I thought this tradition confusing and vulgar, but I quickly learned to accept it as the proper performance practice. It was only when I worked at the Rossini Festival in Pesaro that I learned that this practice is indeed vulgar and also unstylistic. Their resident musicologist, the late Philip Gossett (and continued in our own time by *bel canto* specialists such as Will Crutch-field and Anthony Barrese), insisted that the vocal lines be ornamented in such a way as to increase motion as the double bar approached, rather than taking a hiatus and belting out a high note. This increased the excitement of the affect while eliminating its circus aspect, thereby providing a satisfying alternative for both singer and audience.

It should be noted that some of the traditional interpolated high notes often became the single highest priority when casting the opera, at the expense of role as written by the composer. The most egregious example is the role of Manrico in *Il Trovatore*, which Verdi composed for dramatic tenor (as evinced by its low tessitura). It is rare for a dramatic tenor to possess a ringing high C, which is the note interpolated in Manrico's cabaletta "Di quella pira." After the tradition took hold, opera houses were often guilty of casting the role on the basis of a tenor's high C, generally at the expense of the role itself, which requires a more dramatic sound, to the detriment of the opera.

The Strauss example cited above is an example of a composer wanting to showcase the strength of a certain singer in a single instance. With this, performers can justify singing it as written, or as the composer himself performed it.

The final category is the transposition of sections of an opera to accommodate a particular singer, whether sanctioned by the composer or not. Strauss transposed much of the baritone role of Mandryka in *Arabella* lower in order to make it possible for the legendary bass Hans Hotter to essay the role. Mozart himself had the orchestra parts of the Donna Elvira's "Mi tradi" transposed down a half step, which makes it possible for mezzo sopranos to sing the role. The challenge for the singer or conductor who would like to follow the composer's precedent is to locate orchestral materials for the transpositions. On the other hand, Wagner's lowering of "Traft ihr das Schiff" and Bellini's lowering of "Casta diva" made their way into the published scores, resulting in those becoming the standard performance keys (though the standard transposition of the duet "Mira, o Norma" is in the orchestral parts but not in the piano-vocal score). Transposition of arias (either up or down) to show off the strengths of singers was such a common practice in the nineteenth and early twentieth centuries that the skill of transposing at sight was a requirement for all musicians playing in opera orchestras of that time. Randy Mickelson related to me that upon looking through the orchestra parts in the library of the San Carlo opera house at Naples, he saw scribbled in pencil above an aria: "Monday: e minor"; "Tuesday: d minor"; "Wednesday: e flat minor"; etc., in order to accommodate the various singers in a performance run. Undoubtedly some orchestra musicians would occasionally forget the day of the week, and cacophony would ensue. Rosa Ponselle's flawless recording of "Sempre libera" has her singing the famous cabaletta in G flat major (i.e., a whole tone lower than the published score).

The question remains: Which traditions should be retained as valid and desirable, and which should be jettisoned as obsolete vestiges of the past? If we base our decisions on the composers' wishes (either specific or extrapolated from), we will not be led astray.

The first category would clearly be valid as a way to facilitate the singer's ability to communicate the text while sounding beautiful. While we may not have the composers' blessing, we could easily argue our case as serving the music and the text.

Composer-sanctioned cuts should not trouble anyone. Those made for the sake of economy could easily be argued as being a necessary evil, yet preferable to not producing a masterpiece due to certain overtime orchestral costs or geared to the attention spans of a local audience.

The third category of interpolated high notes, especially when preceded by a hiatus in the vocal line, is a more complicated issue. Clearly, this tradition is not based on musical values but on sporting values. But who is willing to hazard the wrath of an audience who may have come with specific expectations? Even Maria Callas herself was not willing to take such a risk (see chapter 12: "Maria Callas: Self-Effacing Purist"). The solution might be in the historically correct practice of substituting a different kind of visceral excitement for those formerly obtained by untasteful interpolated high notes, by increasing motion toward the double bar.

Finally, the practice of singing arias in keys other than those published (especially those not condoned by the composer) is not only out of fashion, but it is considered unacceptable by audiences and by nearly all conductors. There are exceptions to this rule, such as Dappertuto's

"Scintille, diamant" and Rodolfo's "Che gelida manina," in which alternate keys are included in the orchestral parts. It is my belief that this practice would make a welcome comeback to the benefit of singers, audiences, and the music were a mechanism to be found to transpose the orchestral materials inexpensively.

Whose interpretation of tradition in music is correct: Mahler's or Fleming's? While many of these choices are the province of the conductor, surprisingly many are potentially negotiable. One should always assume that you want what is best both for the music and for your audience.

Professional Artistic Collaboration Strategies

TALKING WITH CONDUCTORS

You think the conductor is there to make you look good. The conductor thinks you are there to make him look good. While neither may be the case, you cannot go wrong by starting with this premise. While many conductors may assume that the singers are there solely to bring their musical vision to life, many will also allow you to penetrate and reshape this vision if you prove yourself worthy. This can be achieved by gaining his or her confidence and admiration from the start of rehearsal one. If you arrive ultra-prepared both musically and vocally, you will exude a well-earned confidence. If this confidence is balanced by humility and an eagerness to learn and grow, you will have a chance at being considered an artistic partner of the conductor, worthy of respect.

Once you have an inkling that the conductor may approve of your singing and/or of your artistry, you may then be in a position to negotiate musically if you have something you feel strongly about, and if there is sufficient rehearsal time available. At that point, you might ask for a private coaching on the role, where you can make a case for your interpretation without others being present. If you do not feel strongly, or if rehearsal time is tight, suppress your will and defer. A good rule is to always be ready and willing to defer: The conductor has the power to expose or hide your weak points to your audience. You need him as an ally, rather than as an adversary.

Once in your coaching, be strategic and prioritize. Know exactly what you would like to accomplish musically, and be ready to defend your viewpoint musically. Use the tools you have acquired through your analysis of the score. If you would like to linger longer on a high note than the conductor has allowed you to, you might ask humbly, "Would you consider allowing me more time on this high note, if I promise to continue the musical impulse to here?" Some conductors are willing to consider dramatic reasons for musical choices, while others are not. Begin with the language you know they speak—i.e., the music. Nearly all conductors are willing to entertain musical reasons for musical choices from intelligent, well-prepared singers. Feel free to test the waters, but always be willing to defer. Never should your reason be "I feel it this way." Here I quote the legendary maestro Riccardo Muti: "My answer to people who say, 'I feel it like this,' would be, 'Get lost! There is no "I feel it like this!"'"[1] Nor would it be in your best interest to say, "I need xxx," thereby leaving the conductor with the impression that you are not up to the demands of the role. A more successful approach might be to say: "Maestro, would you consider helping me here by doing xxx?" With that approach, you are inducing him to be your musical partner, rather than laying down the law. Whenever possible, let him own his authority. Under no circumstances should you correct him, as you have nothing to gain and much to lose by doing so.

This reminds me of a story told to me by a well-known tenor who arrived at his first rehearsal for Verdi's *Un ballo in maschera* with an equally well-known conductor. When they arrived at the tenor's first aria, the conductor announced to all present: "You don't know *Ballo*, I know *Ballo*." The tenor thereupon said, "I have sung in eight productions of *Ballo*, including at theatres x, y, and z." The conductor, who had listened patiently, responded to the tenor with "I know *Ballo*, you don't know *Ballo*." The wise tenor did not take the bait, and proceeded to sing exquisitely, following every gesture of the conductor's baton. They ultimately became great colleagues, with the conductor requesting the tenor whenever he could.

TALKING WITH STAGE DIRECTORS

When interacting with the stage director, start with the same assumptions as for the conductor. In our time, the stage directors often outrank the conductors in the eyes of management, so that relationship is of particular importance. The biggest difference between the language you use with your stage director and the language you use with your conductor is that with the former, you should gear your discussion to the text and your characterization, whereas with the latter, you should speak the language of the music. Do not assume that your stage director reads music, since many, even at the highest level of the industry, do not. To point out things in the score might make them defensive, so it should be avoided. If you want to discuss something about the staging and characterization that you feel is supported by the music, it is always best to ask if the stage director is hearing what you are hearing, rather than telling them what they should be hearing! If you need help with practical matters, like being able to see the conductor's cue or beat at a certain spot, tell the director what your goal is, rather than offering a solution. (The director may prefer to set up a video monitor for you than to provide you with a clear view of the conductor.) If you are asked to sing in an awkward position that impedes your vocalism, tell the stage director what the problem is and perhaps ask if the two of you can search for a solution together. Again, you want to be seen as a partner rather than an inhibitor.

TALKING WITH YOUR HARPSICHORDIST OR CONTINUO GROUP LEADER

If the harpsichordist or continuo group leader is someone other than the conductor, you are probably more or less on the same level in the power structure of the production. That may make collaboration easier, but do not assume that will be the case: You may need to win him or her over, as you would the conductor and stage director. It is worth the trouble, since they can help you shine or can easily take away your luster. Please read my story about Tatiana Troyanos (in chapter 3: "Ornamentation and Recitative") as an illustration of an ideal invitation to collaborate artistically.

Interacting with Your Singer Colleagues

There are some simple rules for establishing and maintaining good relationships with your singer colleagues. First and foremost, never tell them how they should be doing their job: Leave that to the conductor and stage director. Secondly, never tell any of your colleagues how they could sing better. Even if they ask for your opinion, they do not want to know: They only want your assurance that they are terrific. Never tell them otherwise, even if it means telling a lie. Should your colleague corner you after they have sung a high C that cracked obviously and painfully, asking whether you heard it, reply that it was as lovely as ever. Here is an opportunity to test your acting skills. Thirdly, come to rehearsals with your music thoroughly prepared. It is a sign of respect to your colleagues, to the conductor and stage director, and ultimately to yourself. If you are fumbling for your notes, rhythms, or words, you are sending the message to your colleagues that because of your superiority, you think that it is fine for the rehearsal process to be stalled because of your laziness and inconsideration. They will pretend to be patient and understanding, but they will resent and hate you for it.

As a summary, in all professional situations as well as in nonprofessional situations, treat others as you like to be treated. Kindness and consideration always reap great rewards, and apologies cost you nothing.

Audition Strategies

Now it's time to make use of the skills you have acquired from this book. If presented properly, your auditions should garner you more positive feedback than before.

Here are some things to consider:

The people you are auditioning for are trying to ascertain in just a few minutes whether you are someone they would like to spend six-plus weeks with, usually cooped up in a windowless underground rehearsal room. They begin by judging the personality you project as you enter the room. First impressions are important. Look put-together, like you care about your appearance, without appearing vain. Do not dress in a sexually provocative manner. Dressing neatly is a sign of respect that will be noted. You want to present yourself as a person who is comfortable in your own skin. Because we have judged hundreds of auditions and competitions, it is surprisingly easy for us to see who is comfortable with themselves by the way they walk into a room.

Be friendly, but not flirtatious. Introduce yourself with confidence but avoid cockiness. Know your worth and own it! Don't be afraid to smile. If you walk past the judges, stop to introduce yourself to them directly, looking into their eyes, one at a time. Shake their hands if that seems appropriate.

When you arrive at the performance area, begin by quietly explaining to the pianist anything that needs explaining (the less, the better). Then announce clearly to the judges what you would like to begin with, including the title of the aria, the name of the opera, and in all but the most obvious instances, the name of the composer as well. Project the same openness and friendliness as you did when you introduced yourself. Next, drop your head for a few moments with your eyes closed to compose yourself. Then open your eyes and raise your head in the character that you are about to portray. Communicate the emotion of what you are about to sing by the speed at which you raise your head. (For a joyful, infectious aria, you will undoubtedly raise your head much more quickly than for a sad, introspective one.) The greater the difference between that character and your own, the better. Do not tell the pianist when to begin playing. They should easily be able to read your intention to begin by the way you raise your head. If they are unable to read your intention, the fault is yours. If they have not begun playing after an uncomfortable amount of time, turn to them and say, "I'm sorry. I'm ready whenever you are." Never, under any circumstances, berate the pianist. You will only succeed in convincing the jury that you are someone they do not want to know.

If you are asked to sing another aria, it is always preferable to announce the names of the other arias you have prepared, rather than handing out a typed menu as you enter. Any opportunity to interact with the judges is a gift you should seize. Once the next aria has been chosen, repeat the process of dropping your head for a moment of calm before inhabiting the next character.

One attribute that is always welcome is for you to project that you love making music with your voice. This is infectious, and entire superstar careers have been based on it.

Always make sure that your music is complete, legible, and the pages are in the proper order for the pianist. The bass line of the final staff must not be omitted. This is all your responsibility, and if you ignore it, you will not get hired because the pianist will not be able to show you off. After all your study, not tending to your audition book is an unconscious means of sabotaging your career prospects.

Self-Effacing Purist

Maria Callas

Of all of the great singers since recordings existed, Maria Callas best exemplifies the approach I advocate with regard to using musical and textual analysis as the building blocks of the construction of your characters. Callas possessed a voice of seemingly limitless coloration that she utilized in the service of artistic expression. She changed colors to project character and motivation without ever intentionally sacrificing technique or vocal beauty, except when she felt that the characterization necessitated it.

I would describe her instrument as a dramatic mezzo-soprano: weighty and thick in the middle with an extension at both ends. Through perseverance and discipline, and with the aid of her teacher, Elvira de Hidalgo, a celebrated coloratura soprano herself, she willed herself to be the most important singer of the soprano *bel canto* repertory of her time.

My description of Callas as a self-effacing purist may fly in the face of everything you have heard and read about Maria Callas. I will not delve into her personal life or analyze her persona; nor will I discuss the damage that occurred to her instrument and speculate what may have caused it. What is important and relevant here is to discuss Maria Callas's methodology as an artist, and one to emulate.

When considering Callas in the *bel canto* repertoire, it must be remembered that she came of age in a time when come è scritto was the ideal; when reverence toward the printed page was everything. It is highly unlikely that she knew Manuel Garcia's contemporary performance practice writings on Rossini, Donizetti, and Bellini (see chapter 4: "The *bel canto* composers"). As a product of her times and by natural inclination, her attitude toward ornamentation was that of a musical purist. Here is what her friend and biographer John Ardoin reported: "Her taste kept embellishments to a minimum, organic and harmonically suitable. She and conductor Gianandrea Gavazzeni once seriously considered giving Lucia exactly as written with no embellishments, even to cutting the famous cadenza of the Mad Scene. Though both were excited by the cleanliness and force of the idea, it was abandoned out of fear that audience and critics would not understand their reasons."[1] Presumably it was her interest in returning the focus to the composer that caused Callas to consider wiping the Lucia score clean of all traditional cadenzas and ornaments that had accreted to it in the century or more since its composition. It was only when she realized that by doing so, the focus would be turned on her, rather than on Donizetti, that she abandoned the idea. Her motives were reverence toward the music. Had Callas known conclusively that Donizetti expected and encouraged his singers to be active collaborators in performance, she might have embellished the music liberally. Her priority was reverence for the score, tempered by what she perceived to be correct performance practice.

In interviews with Edward Downes in 1967 and 1968, Callas clarified what the term *bel canto* meant to her: "*Bel canto* means great schooling, the exact schooling that each instrumentalist must go through. No matter how dramatically you sing, the *bel canto* must exist. It is not beautiful singing, it is how you sing: the approach. . . . The pure attack of the note is the basis of *bel canto*. Years and years of dominating the voice to do what an instrumentalist would do, you have to do with the voice; absolutely, whether you sing Wagner or anything under the sun."[2]

Callas's characterizations were often triggered by a naïve or obvious fact. Conductor Nicola Rescigno once asked her, after their performance of the final scene from *Anna Bolena* in concert, why she had shaped a certain phrase in a certain manner. "Because she is a queen," Callas replied with little elaboration. This bare idea was enough in itself to set her imagination coursing in a new and different direction than it had with Lucia or Norma. Callas never intellectualized a role, because to do so would have involved working apart from the score with facts that could not be translated into musical terms. The whole Callas mechanism was sparked by music. Once she understood the nature of a character in simple terms—"queen" or "gypsy," "priestess" or "peasant"—she grafted this kernel of thought to what she found within the music. That a prismatic characterization evolved in the process is beyond explanation.

Callas said, "Now history has its Anna Bolena, which is quite different from Donizetti's. Donizetti made her a sublime woman, a victim of circumstance, nearly a heroine. I couldn't bother with history's story: it really ruined my insight. I had to go by the music, by the libretto. The music itself justifies it, so the main thing is not the libretto, though I give enormous attention to the words. I try to find truth in the music. You take this music and you learn it as if you were in the conservatory; in other words, exactly as it is written, nothing more and nothing less. It is what I call 'straightjacketing.' The conductor gives you his cuts, his possibilities, ideas about what his cadenzas might be—and his cadenzas are never his if he is a conscientious conductor, he always builds his cadenzas according to the taste and particular nature of the composer—Bellini is quite different from Donizetti, and Donizetti is different from Rossini. We must use these embellishments to the service of expression. If you care for the composer and not for your own personal success, you will always find an embellishment, trill, or scale that justifies an expression, a feeling of happiness or unhappiness, anxiety."[3]

In an interview with John Ardoin in 1968,[4] Callas recounted her reaction to hearing a playback of a recording session: "I was in quite good voice that day, for you know we have our ups and downs. I was proud when I stepped down to listen to the playback and I told our then artistic director Walter Legge, 'That was, I think, some good singing.' 'Oh, extraordinary,' he said, 'but now you will hear it and you will understand that you have to redo it.' I was a bit shocked and said, 'What do you mean by that?' He said, 'You'll listen to it and you'll see.' In fact, I did listen to it, and it was astonishing, perfect vocally. But the main idea of this Sleepwalking Scene was not underlined. In other words, she is in a nightmare-sleepwalking stage. She has to convey all these off thoughts which go through her head—evil, fearsome, terrifying. So I had made a masterpiece of vocal singing, but I had not done my job as an interpreter. Immediately, as soon as I heard it, I said, 'Well, you are right: now I understand.' And I went and performed it."

Callas continued, "You see, I think she must have at least six mental thoughts that come to her here, one completely different from the other. For she has reached a state of mind that is, shall we say, conscience. She is a very ambitious lady, and for the sake of her vanity, she has persuaded her husband to kill the king so he could become king. Disaster has come because she could not stand her guilt and went mad. She finally copes with her madness in this Sleepwalking Scene. A mad person, of course, has one thought into another without continuity. One minute she is talking about the bloodstains on her hands, terrified that she can never get them clean, and right away she says, 'Come now, we must get ready to receive these people; everything is fine.' All of a sudden, she comes back to another mental attitude. So you cannot perform it with only one line from beginning to end. You have to break it into every one of her thoughts." She then continues to analyze the text of the aria line by line and thought by thought. She concludes: "How can a madwoman with crazy thoughts jumping from one to the other be conveyed in a straight, lovely kind of evenly placed vocal piece? It cannot. Therefore I had to break it into all these pieces, and Verdi helps a singer so with all his diminuendos, crescendos, and allargandos."

This, then, is the key to the art of Maria Callas, a method of inquiry that can and should be emulated by all singers. At some point in her study, she analyzed the text in light of the entire arc of the character, deciding where each thought began and ended, and related it to the character's emotional state at the moment. She let the music guide her in her decision making, both in its broader structure and in its details. Callas never made her musical choices based on what made her sound best; instead she made her vocalism serve the text and music as best she could. Her approach to music was that of a purist, and her interpretative choices were all about the music and the text—self-effacing rather than self-serving.

We can learn from Callas's own thoughts about interpretation: "Music is not composed only for the beauty of it; it has a reason. Every note and every word has a reason, stage-wise and expression-wise. Every detail is written to express a particular emotion. You have to stage first with the voice, then the gesture, if necessary. . . . When we perform, the first person we must respect and the first person we serve is the composer, according to what you think he wanted, you make it your own according to his style."[5]

IV

Six Example Analyses

1 3

Six Example Analyses

"Mi chiamano Mimì," from *La Bohème* by Puccini

Sì. Mi chiamano Mimì,	Yes. They call me Mimì,
ma il mio nome è Lucia.	But my [real] name is Lucia.
La storia mia è breve.	My history is brief
A tela o a seta	Onto cloth or silk
ricamo in casa e fuori . . .	I embroider at home or elsewhere . . .
Son tranquilla e lieta	I am peaceful and happy
ed è mio svago	And my pastime
far gigli e rose.	Is to make lilies and roses.
Mi piaccion quelle cose	I like those things
che han sì dolce malìa,	That have a sweet fragrance,
che parlano d'amor, di primavere,	That speak of love, of spring,
di sogni e di chimere,	of dreams, and of chimeras,
quelle cose che han nome poesia . . .	These things that have poetic names . . .
Lei m'intende?	Am I making sense?

95

Mi chiamano Mimì,	They call me Mimì:
il perché non so.	I don't know why.
Sola, mi fo	Alone, I make
il pranzo da me stessa.	Lunch for myself.
Non vado sempre a messa,	I don't always go to mass,
ma prego assai il Signore.	But I pray.
Vivo sola, soletta	I live alone, entirely alone
là in una bianca cameretta:	Up there in a little white room
guardo sui tetti e in cielo;	I look onto rooftops and to heaven.
ma quando vien lo sgelo	By when the thaw comes
il primo sole è mio	The first sun is mine,
il primo bacio dell'aprile è mio!	The first kiss of April belongs to me!
Germoglia in un vaso una rosa . . .	A rose buds in a vase . . .
Foglia a foglia la spio!	Petal by petal, I watch it!
Cosi gentile il profumo d'un fiore!	That sweet perfume of a flower!
Ma i fior ch'io faccio,	But the flowers that I make
Ahimè! non hanno odore.	Alas, they have no fragrance!
Altro di me non le saprei narrare.	I don't know what else to say about myself.
Sono la sua vicina che la vien fuori	I am your neighbor who came unexpectedly to
und'ora a importunare	bother you.

Tr. Neal Goren

As always when you begin studying any new piece, begin with a quick scan of the text, then return later to puzzle over the details.

A quick scan of the text reveals two important things about Mimì and her character: Firstly, her sense of isolation is palpable, and she keeps returning to it, perhaps in spite of herself. It is the recurring motive of her life summary. Second of all (and surely related to the first), she's obviously unaccustomed to talking about herself: She has no idea what's appropriate to reveal about herself on first meeting. The evidence of this is that she presents her biography to Rodolfo in fits and starts, not in the logical, continual manner of someone who has done this before. And what she omits is at least as significant as what she includes: She does not mention where she is from, when and why she came to Paris, and who her friends are. Any normal person would include these essential facts in a thumbnail sketch of their background, yet she does not. She presents herself a woman without a past, and with only a vague present. And while trying to stick to the facts, she twice retreats into expressing her inner life (beginning with "*Mi piaccion . . .*," then again with "*ma quando vien lo sgelo . . .*"), then snaps out of it and returns to her present conversation with Rodolfo. This is clearly a young woman who has spent too much time alone and is unaccustomed to socializing in even the most basic manner.

A picture emerges of a highly vulnerable, deeply lonely young woman who has espied an attractive young man and his seemingly fun friends from her window above. She has certainly heard them from the hallway (as we did when they left him earlier in the act), and probably through the ceiling as well. In her loneliness, she has probably already constructed her own version of who they are from what she has seen and the snippets of what she has heard. As the stage director Bernard Uzan pointed out to me, she must have assembled these impressions quickly, or else Rodolfo and his friends would have certainly run into her had they shared the same staircase for long.

From this cursory scan of the text, we can (rightly) conclude that Mimì knows that she needs to be part of a social circle and desperately wants to enter into Rodolfo's, because it is both alluring and convenient. Mimì possesses enough self-knowledge to write her own prescription to ameliorate her present circumstances. She needs connection to others her own age, and they just happen to be right on the other side of her door.

As for Rodolfo, he has probably deduced that someone has been living below, but he's never heard conversation to confirm this because there hasn't been any. Let us hope and assume that Mimì does not talk to herself, in spite of her vivid inner life.

Now that we have learned what we can about Mimì from the text of the aria, let us go back and analyze the text in relation to the music. The first thing she says is "*Sì.*" What is she responding affirmatively to? If we turn back a page of the score, we see that Rodolfo has just sung his aria, "*Che gelida manina*" to Mimì, concluding with "Now that you know all about me, tell me who you are. Please do." Her response to his exhortation is a non-sequitur, as he has not asked a question that requires a yes-or-no answer. While her "yes" may be interpreted as "yes, I will," it could equally be an actual non-sequitur that betrays her nervousness and discomfort at the prospect of talking about herself. What might she be nervous about? Being thought stupid perhaps, or, more likely, nervous about the possibility of blowing her chance at finding friends and allaying her loneliness. For Mimì, the stakes are quite high. Notice that there is a rest after she says "Yes." She has not had time to consider what she will say next after agreeing to speak, so she takes a breath to consider where to begin. Her first two lines are delivered together, so we can deduce that her nickname and her name are one fact to her, not two. Or if you'd prefer to raise the stakes, perhaps she generally keeps her real name secret, but at the spur of the moment (after saying "yes") she makes a quick calculation and decides to share this personal intimacy with the handsome upstairs neighbor who shows an interest in her and can provide her with a community.

Then there is a full beat of silence before she continues. It seems like quite a long time, and it should. She does not know how to proceed. She eventually admits that she doesn't have much to say, but she nonetheless leaves out all important facts about her past. After she divulges her employment as an embroiderer, she again is at a loss for words. This time there is a painfully long fermata over the rest before she continues. When she begins again, she talks about her nature ("I am peaceful and happy"), which she offers lest Rodolfo get the impression that she might be a needy, unhappy person, and she mentions her hobby, which keeps her occupied, lest he conclude that she has too much free time on her hands.

After these calculated attempts to dispel any warning signs that she may have unintentionally set off in Rodolfo's mind, she begins her first reverie. For someone who is concerned about the impression she is making, it is odd that she allows herself to retreat into her head without taking time to consider the ramifications. Either she cannot control herself, which is entirely possible for someone who has spent too much time alone, or knowing that Rodolfo is a poet, she thinks he may be captivated enough by an occasional flight of fancy to identify her as a kindred spirit.

Her bet proves to be correct. When she asks for his approval and receives it, she feels emboldened to continue, but not knowing what to say, she begins anew, this time expressing her ignorance at the origin of her nickname (and, if we follow Puccini's staccatti, her embarrassment). She then perceives sufficient interest and trust emanating from Rodolfo to continue to list her solitary activities: eating alone, praying alone, and finally living alone. Some sopranos have delivered this latter fact with a wink, to let Rodolfo know that she is unchaperoned and available. I don't buy it. She is after long-term friendship (though she proves to be open to love), and her need for community is too strong (might I say desperate?) to angle for merely short-term relief.

After describing her simple quarters, she unselfconsciously launches into her second reverie, much longer than the first. When she snaps out of it, she is embarrassed and chatters nervously, apologizing for her intrusion, undoubtedly hoping for a conciliatory reaction to her apology, when they are interrupted by the very friends she longs to know.

We soon learn that she can offer him what he needs as much as he can offer her what she needs, and they both sense this immediately. She needs someone to make her feel safe, and he needs to feel able to protect someone. That's why they are able to fall in love so quickly, practically instantaneously. And they are able to fulfill each other's needs until the bar gets raised through no fault of their own.

Renata Scotto expressed to me her opinion that this is not really an aria, but a soliloquy. It cannot be argued that there is no musical or narrative arc to it. It is, certainly, one of the most touching explorations of a vulnerable, modest character in opera, and it is up to you to convey that to your audience. It would be possible but misguided to portray Mimì as manipulative, but perfectly accurate to portray her as strategic.

"SE COME VOI PICCINA," FROM *LE VILLI* BY PUCCINI

Se come voi piccina,	If I were tiny like you,
io fossi, o vaghi fior,	O charming flowers,
sempre, sempre vicina	then I could always, always stay close
potrei stare al mio amor.	to my love.
Allor dirgli vorrei	Then I would tell him:
"Io penso sempre, sempre a te!"	"I'm always, always thinking of you!"
Ripeter gli potrei	I could say to him
Non ti scordar di me!	Forget me not!
Io penso sempre, sempre a te!	I'm always, always thinking of you!
Non ti scordar di me,	Forget me not!
non ti scordar di me!	Forget me not!
non ti scordar,	Do not forget,
non ti scordar di me!	Forget me not!
No! no! no! no!	No! No! No! No!
Non ti scordar di me!	Forget me not!
Voi, di me più felici,	Now you, happier than I,
lo seguiterete, o fior;	will follow him, O flowers;

per valli e per pendici	over hills and dales,
seguirete il mio amor . . .	you will follow my love . . .
Ah, se il nome che avete	Ah, if the name you bear
Menzognero non è,	is not false,
Deh! al mio amor ripetete:	then tell my love:
"Non ti scordar di me!	"Forget me not!
Ah! non ti scordar,	Ah! Do not forget,
non ti scordar,	Do not forget,
non ti scordar di me,	Forget me not,
non ti scordar di me,	Forget me not,
non ti scordar,	Do not forget,
non ti scordar di me!	Forget me not!
No! no! no! no!	No! No! No! No!
non ti scordar di me!"	Forget me not!"

Tr. Neal Goren and Francis Keeping

Even before studying the text of the aria, it would be wise to translate its title. Since "Villi" is not in any Italian-English dictionary, you must engage in a bit of research to discover your answer. Puccini based his opera on a French short story titled *Les Willis* by Alphonse Karr, whose title was translated into Italian as *Le Villi*. This story was itself based on a Central European legend of the Vila, a race of beautiful, dangerously seductive women who can change themselves into various animal forms. In the opera and in Karr's short story, the *Villi/Willis* are vengeful female ghosts who have been betrayed in life by their lovers.

Turning to the text of the aria, what jumps out are the multiple repetitions of the phrase *"Non ti scordar di me,"* or "Don't forget me." Indeed, this phrase is repeated fourteen times in various permutations in the course of the aria.

The opera opens with an engagement party in honor of Anna and Roberto. We learn that Roberto must go on a journey to claim an inheritance that will make them both wealthy. Anna has collected a bouquet of—what else?—forget-me-nots, to remind him of her during his journey.

The great challenge of this aria is how to motivate the text repetitions to make the aria dramatically compelling. The challenge is so daunting that I have never heard a singer even try to make the aria anything other than a ravishing vocalise. I maintain that Puccini deserves more.

Continuing your research, you will learn that later in the opera, Roberto indeed proves to be faithless, Anna dies of a broken heart, and her ghost lures him into the woods to be preyed upon by the Villis. This is a rare instance in which knowing what unfolds later can help motivate the aria, though this knowledge will merely confirm artistic choices that can be made without it.

The singer should start by imagining subtexts for repeating the phrase "Don't forget me!" so many times. Some productions leave Anna to sing this aria to the flowers alone, which makes the aria exceedingly difficult to motivate convincingly. When presenting this aria in concert or in an audition, it will make your challenge lighter if you imagine that you are addressing Roberto himself from time to time, instead of just the flowers themselves. For our purposes, let us imagine he is with the singer. Anna could be simply requesting, or she could be begging, or even threatening. She could be pleading in desperation, or she could be chiding, or warning Roberto with this phrase. There are undoubtedly more possibilities, and all should be considered. The more aggressive choices make sense, knowing that Roberto ultimately proves to be unfaithful, and she senses this potentiality in him already. You might also consider the placement of quotation marks within the text (carefully reproduced above). You may also choose to make this affect your dramatic choices.

Now that you have considered many valid motivations for delivering the much-repeated phrase, you can set about to plan your own personal emotional architecture for the aria, based on the way you order your choices. There is no right and no wrong choice beyond what you feel works best for you and for the aria. The only sin is to be boring and uncommunicative. Remember that Italian composers and audiences of this period had a strong preference for raw emotions, versus effete ones. Anna and Roberto are both hot-blooded peasants. To allow her to be a simpering victim goes against the sensibility of the period. I would also caution against too much specificity in your interpretation, or you will hazard singing the aria while trying to remember which motivation comes next. Better to plan a basic emotional map that makes sense to you and you can follow without undue distraction.

You should also ask yourself: What is the intent of the playful, yet slightly sinister music that introduces the aria and returns between its two verses? Perhaps it is Sara's imagined version of the Villi themselves, or of their dance. It is incumbent upon you to motivate this music as well, and not look blankly bovine when it is being played. Better yet, you should be so expressive that we perceive that this music is coming from you. That should always be your goal, and many great artists have been able to achieve it. If others can do it, so can you!

"ALL'AFFLITTO E DOLCE IL PIANTO," FROM *ROBERTO DEVEREUX* BY DONIZETTI

For a prototype on how to approach a new aria, let's use Sara's aria, "All'afflitto," which opens Donizetti's opera *Roberto Devereux*. I have chosen this aria because it is brief, neither standard nor obscure, and it should elicit the same types of questions as every other aria you will study throughout your career.

As always, let's begin with the text:

All'afflitto è dolce il pianto	To the sufferer, crying (pain) is sweet
E la gioia che gli resta . . .	And joy is in what remains . . .
Una stella a me funesta	A fatal star
Anche il pianto mi vietò.	Has forbidden my sorrow.
Della tua più cruda, oh quanto,	Oh Rosamonda, my cruel fate
Rosamonda, è la mia sorte!	Is worse than yours!

Tu peristi d'una morte . . .	You perished . . .
Io vivendo ognor morrò.	But I die by living.

Tr. Neal Goren and Francis Keeping

The first question you might ask is, who is Rosamonda? A quick glance at the list of characters in the opera does not include anyone with that name. This should lead you to the internet or the library where you will discover that Rosamonda is the Italian name for Rosamund Clifford, "The Fair Rosamund," a mistress of Henry II of England in the twelfth century. According to legend, Henry, in order to hide this affair from his wife, Eleanor of Aquitaine, arranged for his trysts with Rosamund to occur in the depths of a labyrinth he had constructed for this purpose. When Eleanor heard rumors of these assignations, she cracked the maze and confronted her rival, offering her a choice of death by dagger or by poison. Rosamund chose poison and died.

From the totality of the aria's text, it is now clear that Sara considers her fate to be worse than that of Rosamund, because she is forced to live. You should next ask yourself why she feels this way. Reading ahead in the libretto (or via the internet), you will discover that Sara is in love with Roberto Devereux, who is her husband's closest friend. Therefore, Sara, like the fair Rosamund, is in love with a married man. Sara, unlike Rosamund, is married herself, which makes her situation yet worse than that of Rosamund.

Now we can move on to the music. If not sung too slowly, the first two lines of text could be sung in one breath (mm. 6–10). Donizetti, however, chose to interrupt these two lines by two internal breaths. Though it is impossible for us to know exactly why the composer made this decision, we can conjecture that either Sara is crying or is too overcome by emotion to sing this sentiment in one breath. Or perhaps she is formulating her thoughts as she goes along. If you can come up with an alternate reason for these breaths, all the better! The important thing is that you pose the question to yourself and come to your own conclusion. Looking ahead, Donizetti interrupts the next thought (lines 3 and 4 of the text) with another internal breath. Likewise, the next two lines of text (lines 5–6) he interrupts with two internal breaths (mm. 14–18 in the music). Clearly, Sara is unable to express her thoughts in a straightforward manner.

Moving on, Donizetti repeats the final two lines of the text four times, from which we must conclude that this is the heart of Sara's utterance. The first three times, the text is uninterrupted by internal breaths. One interpretation might be that she pulled herself together temporarily, and another might be that here she formulated a complete thought before expressing it. The final time she sings this text (mm. 26–32), it is interrupted by two written internal breaths (and at least two additional implied breaths), including a cadenza and word repetition. From this concluding extended utterance of this text, we may choose to reject the conjecture that she is singing a complete thought simply because she has formulated it in advance. Or perhaps you could justify this analysis by saying that after singing the line uninterrupted three times, she finally realizes the importance of what she has been saying and can no longer express it simply. These are both valid interpretations, as they are rooted in the text and its musical setting.

In either case, the vocal writing, and hence the emotional architecture of mm. 18–33, is very different from that of the first eighteen measures. Your singing of mm. 6–18 and 26–33 should be at a higher emotional level than that of mm. 18–26, because the composer set it that way (by the inclusion of numerous rests interrupting her thoughts).

Lastly, consider any unexpected harmonies or expressive marks in the music. As for harmonies, m. 17 is over a foreign-looking E flat major chord. Upon reflection, this is merely an unremarkable Neapolitan sixth chord that becomes a German sixth chord, leading to the dominant in measure 18, which allows for the cadenza.

In this edition, the only expression mark is the accent in measure 27, whose effect can be likened to a moan, though you may have an alternate description of its emotional content. The orchestra has an accent marked in measure 17. It is up to the singer whether to add an accent above, and whether to add one in the other musically parallel locations in measures 12 and 19.

"VA! LAISSE COULER MES LARMES!," FROM *WERTHER* BY MASSENET

Va! Laisse couler mes larmes!	Go! Let my tears flow!
elles font du bien, ma chérie!	They [will] do me good, my dear!
Les larmes qu'on ne pleure pas	The tears that one does not shed
Dans notre âme retombent toutes,	fall again, all of them, within our soul,
et de leurs patientes goutes	And their patient drops
Martèlent le coeur triste et las.	Hammer the sad and weary heart.
Sa résistance enfin s'épuise;	Its resistance ultimately is spent;
le coeur se creuse et s'affaiblit;	The heart hollows out and weakens;
il est trop grand, rien ne l'emplit;	It [the heart] is too big; nothing fills it;
et trop fragile, tout le brise . . .	And too fragile, everything breaks it . . .
Tout le brise!	Everything breaks it!

Tr. Neal Goren

This aria is one of the wonders of the entire operatic repertoire, and a gift to every mezzo soprano. In it, Charlotte breaks though her emotional frigidity and allows herself to feel pain and remorse.

In the music, the rest between the first word and the sentence that follows is too brief for it to be an entirely new thought. Though these two sentiments ("please get out of here" and "I need to cry") may seem to not belong together, they erupt almost simultaneously after the super-poignant saxophone introduction. This introduction must be perceived as a mirror of your thoughts, so you must be clear with yourself what those thoughts might be. The music expresses the thoughts that are about to erupt from Charlotte, because she can no longer suppress her thoughts, any more than she can suppress her tears. After this emotional outpouring, Massenet gives her four beats of rest, followed by a quiet entrance. Something important must occur in those intervening four beats. Since the next line is an outgrowth of the preceding line, those beats of rest are not there for Charlotte to compose her next thought. If instead you use those beats for Charlotte to get her emotions under control, you will have found the key to her character. Charlotte, either by upbringing or by temperament, does not want to be a highly emotional woman. She sees herself as someone who can keep her unwanted emotions in check by force of her will. We soon learn that she is deceiving herself, and she eventually realizes it too. But at this moment the audience members are just beginning to realize how willful she is, and how terrified she is of her emotions. All that follows is self-justification. The two intervening measures of rest after "elles font du bien, ma chérie!" can be infused with more self-repression; with Charlotte's searching for self-justification; or for needing the time to formulate her next thought; or with self-loathing for having lost control of herself, especially in front of her younger sister; or any combination of the four. Or perhaps you can find another reason why Massenet gave Charlotte all that time before expressing the next thought, fully formed, to her sister. Until "le coeur se creuse et s'affaiblit," the rests are very poised and do not need to carry great emotional baggage. The musical sequence of measures 17 and 18 express a quick building up of emotion, in spite of the rhythmic repetition occurring at a lower pitch. Perhaps this expresses the conflict within Charlotte, both needing to give vent to her emotions, yet wanting to suppress them.

Note that the following phrase, "le coeur," is delayed by rests and is introduced by the shortest note value we have heard thus far, as is the next phrase, "se creuse." Clearly she does not want to say these words or feel these thoughts, yet she cannot help herself. The diminuendo on "et s'affaiblit" indicates that she is again trying to suppress these inconvenient emotions. Thereupon follows, with only the briefest eighth-note rest, her climactic outburst, "the heart is so big, it cannot be filled." Clearly, she has thought this before and finally allows herself to express it, perhaps in spite of herself. After a very long pause during which Charlotte must either compose herself or prepare to explain herself, she admits her fragility in a whisper, again almost in spite of herself. Then she repeats the phrase "tout le brise!" with many essential indications of expression, and you must justify both the word repetition and the expressive indications in order to bring Charlotte to life. As with every other great opera aria, you must make your choices about the character in light of the text and the music, and your choices will determine how the audience perceives her.

"IL LACERATO SPIRITO," FROM *SIMON BOCCANEGRA* BY VERDI

A te l'estremo addio,	My final farewell to you,
Palagio altero,	Proud palace,
Freddo sepolcro dell'angiolo mio!	The cold tomb of my angel!
Nè a proteggerti valsi!	I was unable to protect her!
Oh maledetto! O vile seduttore!	Oh damned one! Oh vile seducer!
E tu, Vergin, soffristi	And you, Virgin Mary, did you stand by
Rapita a lei la verginal corona?	While her crown of virginity was taken?
Ah! Che dissi? Deliro!	Ah! What did I say? I am raving!
Ah, mi perdona!	Ah, forgive me!
Il lacerato spirito del mesto genitore	The wounded spirit of a sad father
Era serbato a strazio d'infamia e dei dolore.	Was kept in the torment of shame and of grief.

Il serto a lei de'martiri pietoso in cielo diè . . .	Pitying heaven gave her a martyr's crown . . .
Resa al fulgor degli angeli,	Restored her to the splendor of the angels,
Prega, Maria, per me.	Pray for me, Mary.

Tr. Neal Goren

Here we have a text of one of the most popular bass arias in the repertoire. The reasons for its popularity are many: It is extremely well written for the voice, it has no high notes, it is not long, and it is inarguably beautiful. But of the hundreds of times I have heard it sung in auditions, I cannot think of a single instance in which a character or a scene was evoked. It is not a huge challenge for a singer to do so, yet it can make the difference between a compelling audition and an ordinary one.

Let us begin by analyzing where each new idea begins in the text. In the first two lines, Fiesco anounces his intention to quit his palace forever. The next piece of information we receive is that his "angel" is entombed therein, which is presumably his reason for leaving. We should note that he gives no clue to the identity of his angel: whether it be his wife, his daughter, his sister, or his mistress. From his lack of specificity, we can deduce that he is speaking solely to himself, and we soon learn that he is raving. Next, we learn that he was unable to protect her from something. But from what? The question is answered in the next line, where we learn that she was seduced by someone damnable.

Now another idea tumbles out. Fiesco accuses the Virgin Mary of allowing the seduction to have taken place: She was asleep at the wheel, as it were. Once he realizes that he is sinning by even thinking such a thing, he is immediately repentant and tries to excuse his reprehensible words by justifying to himself and to the Virgin that he is delirious, presumably from grief.

The remainder of the text of the aria is an expansion of the previous two lines: It is an outpouring of his grief sung over the offstage chorus' quiet confirmation that "She is dead" and their voicing of a Miserere, followed by his plea to the Virgin to grant him peace.

In sum, we have five thoughts in quick succession, followed by two conversations with the Virgin Mary. This is a man who is in such deep anguish that he is casting about for someone to blame for his sorrow. Relief is not forthcoming, which sets the scene for the remainder of the opera.

In order to learn the identity of the "angel," we need to consult the libretto a few pages prior to this soliloquy, in which we learn that it was Fiesco's daughter, Maria, who was seduced and impregnated by the opera's titular character. We also learn that Fiesco would not permit Boccanegra to marry his daughter because he was not of royal blood. Maria therefore died in sin due to her father's pride. His own guilt could account for the enormity of his grief.

Turning to the musical setting of the text, we see that Verdi set the first three lines together as one thought. The two beats of rest that follow signal a new idea that occurs in the rest: an admission of his impotence to prevent the situation that occurred. This is followed by more than five beats of rest in the vocal line that must be filled with emotion to be effective. Here his anger toward his daughter's seducer rises until he curses him. (The high note of the phrase occurs on the word "vile," but the phrase must be directed through to its end, "seduttore," in order to be musically and textually satisfying.) There is another pause following the curse in which Fiesco looks for another object for his blame, which turns out to be the Virgin Mary. The rest is long enough for him to turn his focus to her, but not long enough for him to consider the ramifications of his profane accusation. It is only after uttering this imprecation that he considers the moral implications of what he has just said (indicated by the rising, frantic five-note figures in the orchestra), leading him to regret what he uttered so hastily.

After asking for forgiveness, Fiesco has nearly three measures in which to formulate his defense to the Virgin. When he summons the strength to address her, he is unable to state his case without stopping to catch his breath or perhaps to stifle a sob. When he hears the offstage chorus (and he should hear it), he is led to fantasize that his daughter in heaven is being celebrated as a martyr by the angels. This fantasy is not enough to console him, and during the long intervening silence, he decides to appeal to the Virgin directly—in spite of his recent accusation against her—to accord him peace. It is worth noting that immediately preceding Fiesco's final plea, there occurs one of the few instances, here repeated twice, where Verdi chooses to violate the natural directionality of the language: instead of composing music accentuated "prega per <u>me</u>," he instead sets the text as "<u>prega</u> per me." This is such a rare occurrence in the body of Verdi's work that the singer must consider his reason for doing so. Perhaps after initiating the plea, Fiesco's energy is spent; or perhaps he an old man who is half mumbling to himself; or perhaps Verdi is simply accentuating the desperation of the plea with the addition of the unexpected accent. Other reasons can be found, but it is incumbent on the singer to choose one (or two, since the phrase is repeated exactly) in order to justify this musical oddity. In any event, the accent should be executed leaving no doubt of its presence (see chapter 2: "Where to Begin: Text Analysis and Expression Marks") and whatever artistic intention you have chosen.

This aria is a perfect example of a composition whose effect is entirely dependent on how the singer handles its many rests. If he is able to project the character's inner life and thought process, the rests will be deeply meaningful to the audience. Otherwise, the rests will be vacant, and "the aria will seem meaningless, endless, and lugubrious.

DU BIST WIE EINE BLUME, *LIED* BY SCHUMANN

Now that we have begun to explore how to approach arias to construct a character, let's see whether those tools can serve for song as well. I've chosen Robert Schumann's Du bist wie eine Blume as a protoype, because it is a song that nearly everyone has sung but few have considered, and it is very brief.

Here is Heine's text:

Du bist wie eine Blume	You are like a flower
So hold und schön und rein;	So sweet and fair and pure;
Ich schau' dich an, und Wehmuth	I look at you, and sadness
Schleicht mir in's Herz hinein.	Steals into my heart.

Mir ist, als ob ich die Hände	It seems to me that I should lay my hands
Auf's Haupt dir legen sollt',	Upon your head,
Betend, daß Gott dich erhalte	Praying that God preserve you
So rein und schön und hold.	[Because you're] So pure and fair and sweet.

Tr. Neal Goren

In order to make a satisfying interpretation of this piece, you first must decide what has occurred that moves you to elicit this praise. Has the object of your affection just said or done something to incite you to say/sing this text? Or has something occurred that causes you to compare this person to someone less deserving of praise? Hopefully, the object of praise has not required it of you, as Lear did of his daughters, in order to assess your love.

You must also decide whether you're musing on someone you love or admire, or whether you're speaking directly to that person. If you choose the latter, not only will your performance be more dynamic because something will be at stake, but there will be much more obvious emotional resonance.

Let's say that you choose to sing this text to someone you admire or love. Is this person someone who has demonstrated that your feeling are reciprocated? If so, it will be a lovely song of admiration. If your feelings have not been reciprocated, then you have the choice whether you would like it to be a song of admiration or of seduction. Clearly a song of seduction would be a more dynamic choice, but the choice is up to you: It can be wonderfully effective either way.

Now we can move on to the music itself. Schumann puts a breath between lines 1 and 2. Is the singer relaying a full thought that has occurred to him, or has he said, "You remind me of a flower," and then during the rest he thinks to himself, "Yes, but in what way?" (and there will be a sense of urgency and involvement within the audience that will likewise cause them to ask themselves the same question). Then he proceeds to explain and complete the thought that had occurred to him in line 1. At the end of which, the singer might communicate a sense of relief, or even self-congratulation, for having completed the simile that he had begun. At some point, perhaps, the singer could effectively allow himself to feel that he is on a roll, which gives him the confidence to continue his praise.

Lines 3 and 4 seem like a complete non-sequitur; why should he feel sad when gazing at her/him? There are many possibilities, and each different choice will result in a different song emotionally. Some of those choices might be (1) because the object of affection is taken by another and is prohibited to love, or (2) perhaps simply because this person is so unspeakably exquisite that you are overcome, or (3) that it suddenly strikes you that such beauty and purity cannot remain so forever. Either choose one, or come up with another reason that resonates with you, but you must choose an interpretation. I would encourage you to try more than one on for size with your pianist and see which suits you best and communicates itself best. Avoid taking a breath after "Wehmut," because Schumann has set this irrefutably as a complete thought, unlike the first two lines.

Schumann has begun the second stanza piano, but with the same melody as he introduced the song (minus the breath in the second measure). The dynamic change indicates that this is a new thought, but the identical melody indicates that it is not. Once again, it is up to you to decide. If the singer is making things up as he goes, it will be one thing, but if he is singing one fully considered thought, then it is something else. The former may be more dynamic, while the latter may be the result of a more long-term relationship, where he has had time to consider the object at leisure, and he long made his conclusion. A third, equally valid interpretation is that the second stanza is an outgrowth of the first, but you still have to decide whether the thought has just occurred to you or not. Note the long rest before the final line of text. This needs to hold enough tension that the audience wonders, "Why does the singer pray that God will preserve his object of affection? Is it because of the perfection already mentioned, or will he list another attribute?" You then satisfy their curiosity (provided that you have managed to arouse it in the first place) by repeating one attribute mentioned earlier in line two, and adding another.

Finally, you must decide how to handle the postlude in which you do not sing. As with any musical interlude, your goal should be to make it seem that you are creating the music: that it be heard as a projection of your psyche. If you interpret this Lied as a song of seduction sung to the person before you, you would be nervously awaiting a response after such a heartfelt utterance. Listen to the postlude: It expresses neither joy nor disappointment conclusively, but it is more ambiguous. Once again you get to choose which response you would like to express.

If, on the other hand, you have chosen to interpret this song as a private, intimate disquisition on your love's attributes, then the postlude could be more of a melancholic musing on what you have just sung.

In conclusion, by considering a song in the same way that you consider an aria, you are creating both a character and a world that character inhabits. Du bist wie eine Blume may have initially seemed to you to be a simple little song, but it is a treasure trove of artistic opportunity. Without creating a character, the song is just a pretty melody: Schumann and your audience deserve more.

V

INTERVIEWS WITH
GREAT SINGING ACTORS

CONCLUSIONS FROM, AND AN INTRODUCTION TO, INTERVIEWS

Every successful singer I have encountered has been motivated by a love of music and a need to communicate. If these are not your motivations, I would encourage you to consider a different career: The personal sacrifices are many when building and sustaining a career. If you are motivated by anything other than love of music and the need to communicate, you will be unhappy in this career.

It was only after I finished writing the body of this text that I began my interviews with great singer-actors to see whether their methods for constructing their characters differ from what I have been expounding: namely, that you should begin by reading the text, all the while asking yourself questions about the text, such as: Why is she saying those things? What has led her to react as she is reacting? Is this a new emotion for her, or a familiar one? Is this a new situation for her?

These are only four of the hundreds of questions that should come to you if you are examining the text with the proper level of inquiry. Most of the time, the character you are portraying differs from you in many essential ways. Those are the ways that you should find most interesting to explore and portray.

After you've begun to make decisions for yourself about the character you are to portray (based on the text), you should then study the music to see whether it supports the decisions you have made, or whether you need to reconsider them.

The next step is to go deeper to examine the meaning of every rest, every note, and every expression mark in the music, and decide how these conclusions fill in the gaps in the character decisions that you made solely by reading the text. As obvious as this sounds, your character is the composite of the text and the music and how they relate to you, and it is your job to bring her to life based on those sources.

In the following interviews, you will discover that this method of constructing the character is shared by nearly everyone interviewed, with few exceptions. The most significant divergences between artists comes in the relative value they place on historical research about the times in which the character lived and biographical material pertaining to the character they are portraying (if the character actually existed). Some singers avoid making firm decisions about their character until they get into rehearsals with their stage directors. What is in common between all of the great singing actors interviewed is not only the methodology, but the spirit of joyful inquiry with which they embark on the process. I cannot stress this discovery enough: Every successful artist embraces the process of developing a character through their study of the text and the music, and how they interact. Renata Scotto told me: "In my career, what I enjoyed most of all was studying and working." This is not to say that she did not love performing, but studying and working outranked performing for her. It is the spirit of joy in both learning and performing that communicates itself to the audience and has enabled opera to continue to bring meaning to our lives after four hundred years.

Harolyn Blackwell

Harolyn Blackwell (b. 1955) has had a brilliant career in both opera and musical theater due to her shining lyric-coloratura voice and her charismatic stage presence. She sang leading roles at the Metropolitan Opera, including the title role in *La Fille du Régiment*, as well as Cunegonde in *Candide* on Broadway.

Neal Goren: So, Harolyn, as one of the great singing actresses of our time, I want to know about your process. When you were constructing an unfamiliar character for the first time, did you begin with the text or with the music?

Harolyn Blackwell: I always begin with the text, because I feel that is what the composer starts with, and those are the words we have to convey. So, when you start reading that text as if it's a story, I have found that has helped me in the characterization. So, first and foremost is for me, is the text. So, I start with the text. Just read that through, so I have a sense of where the character is going, the arc of the character, and then go to the source material to fill in the blanks.

When I was doing Gilda for the first time, I felt the need to consult the source material. It really helped me to fill in the blanks, because where you meet her at that point, you wonder, what has happened prior to that?

NG: Right, we never find out.

HB: Exactly. And for me to come to that point where she is in the opera, I have to know what transpired before that. What was her relationship with her mother? How old was she when her mother passed away? I think that's different from an infant, the mother passing away or from even a five or six year old.

NG: Right. So I'm sure you've done some roles where you can't locate the source material. So I guess you have to invent the background for yourself?

HB: Yes, sometimes. Yes, absolutely. But then you still go back to the text because it's there in the text somewhere.

NG: So you begin making your character decisions as you're reading the text, and then you refine it when you go back and reread it?

HB: Exactly. And then you hear it. I mean, a great composer has also done it for you musically.

As I start working on, let's say I'm working on act one, I read the text of act one. Then I'll go back, then the next step is the source material. Then I'll go back and just listen to the act one, and see how musically the words are. The word color is in the music. Because a great composer has done that for you.

NG: So have there ever been any instances where the composer surprised you by the way they set the text?

HB: Yes. That's happened sometimes. And then I feel my job is to go back and figure out why. That's my job, to figure out why did he make this decision. And sometimes it's, again, going back and rereading the text; sometimes it's going back and listening to the music again.

NG: Right. So then do you also ever think about the rests in the music, the length of the rests?

HB: Absolutely. So those rests, sometimes you're thinking, am I singing through those rests or do I need those rests for me to change into another thought about the character?

NG: Exactly.

HB: So for me, what I have learned over the years, even in the silence there is something happening.

NG: Absolutely. Otherwise the audience doesn't care.

HB: Exactly. In the silence there is something happening, so respect that silence. That's been a hard thing for me to do to really respect the silence and go, okay, what is my next thought process to take me to the next step? What I have to do at that moment is to respect the silence and get my intention. Know exactly what my intention is in that silence, and then I'm ready to go.

NG: Excellent. Do you ever take some of these questions and rely on, or at least collaborate with the director or the conductor? If you have some of these questions about the why in a particular passage?

HB: Yes. I mean I think it depends on the director and the conductor I'm working with. Some people are open to that and they will allow you to have this dialogue; I try to have a discussion with them.

NG: Have you ever had one who had a totally different idea than you? Or something that you disagreed with strongly?

HB: I'm trying to think. No, I have to say I haven't, I've been very fortunate in that respect. And I think I found a way to say, "Excuse me maestro, I understand exactly what you're saying. This is, can I sit down and discuss this with you?" I said, "Because I'm feeling this right now, and I want to honor what you're saying. I have to honor what's on the page, what you're saying, but at the same time, what I'm feeling here. And also, which is affecting me vocally." So if my intention is not really right on, it does affect me vocally. If my intention's right on, it's just like it goes, the voice just goes.

NG: Were you always clear about what you wanted to communicate?

HB: Yes. Sitting down doing my homework, yes. And if I wasn't, I would sit down and have a discussion with the director. I think it's mostly because I come from a theater background that I can sit down and discuss these things.

NG: You also have a collaborative personality too.

HB: Yes, I really do. Because it's important to me that it's about all of us getting on that stage and making this work. And if one thing is off, it's not going to work. It just isn't going to work. I remember doing, you know when we did [Mozart's] *The Abduction* [from the *Seraglio*] together, and he didn't give me much, and so I had to really go in there and dig deep and try to find things to really work with what he wanted.

HB: What I came up with made him look good, and made me look good.

NG: Right. So everyone was happy. And the audience was happy too.

HB: Exactly. Because I thought, I can go in this situation and fight him like this, but this is going to be counterproductive. So let's sit down, let's have a discussion, and let's see how we can find that middle ground, what you want, and what I need. And I'm always, I'm a firm believer about the middle ground. You know Neal, it's the same thing about life, as I get older it's not about left, it's not about right. It's trying to find that middle ground.

NG: Can you talk about what the role of vocal technique is in everything else that we discussed?

HB: Well, for me, that's first and foremost. That is first and foremost. For me, if my intentions are so strong, if I know exactly what my intentions are, the vocal technique is right there. What I discovered when I first started out in this business, was that I didn't quite have sufficient vocal technique for what I wanted to communicate. So I had to go back and find the vocal technique, and once I found the vocal technique, that freed me up to express what I wanted to express.

NG: So the vocal technique, with the intention, equals a great performance.

HB: Yes, because I'm telling you, if you don't have that vocal technique, it will not enable you to do what you want to do no matter how much you want to do it or try to do it. But once that technique is solid, then I feel that I can fly like a bird. That I can just, I can soar.

NG: This has been incredibly useful. I thank you so much.

15

Barbara Hannigan

Canadian soprano, **Barbara Hannigan** (b. 1971) is among the leading interpreters of music of our time. Trained both as a singer and as a conductor, she performs worldwide in both capacities. She is a muse to many of today's foremost composers. Hannigan is celebrated for her assumption of the title role of Berg's *Lulu* and for György Ligeti's *Le Grand Macabre*, among numerous others.

Neal Goren: How do you begin to construct a character when you're preparing a work that's new or unfamiliar to you?

Barbara Hannigan: Well, I come at it as blank as possible. I'm not very interested in making any decisions in advance about anything final about who the character is or what her intentions are. I try to stay very, very open. I may make notes, but I intentionally allow them to be contradictory. They're more like options or questions rather than decisions.

NG: Why is that?

BH: It's because I want to stay really clean for all those musical ideas and directorial ideas. I want to stay open to possibilities that I may not have otherwise entertained. That can happen during the process. Sometimes very late in the process I make the decision how I'm going to play something. Yeah, so that's really, really important to me not to get attached to anything. Another thing is that, while I do learn some cues from my colleagues, I don't count on my colleagues being right. It's not that I don't trust other singers, it's that so many things can go wrong. Normally it's much stronger to be attached to the score and the orchestra than it is to be attached to a cue for another voice, because the orchestra will most often be with the conductor, whereas a singer is more likely to be out of synch.

I'm very careful to know the score as well as I can. Then, as I said the other day with Lulu, my interpretation of the character is developed little by little, by wondering, "How does she feel about this line or how did Berg feel about this line? How do I feel about this line?" and kind of gathering a lot of information without pinning anything down. That's really, really important. I put a blank page on the mirror in my dressing room before every performance to just remind me to start from nothing each time. To start really clean.

NG: At each performance, do you feel like you're reinventing?

BH: Yeah, of course, there are agreements that we've made in staging and music, but if something went really well, I don't try to repeat it. If something went badly, I don't fixate on it. It keeps every performance really fresh and spontaneous.

NG: Though of course, some things you have to repeat: the things you've decided along with your director and your conductor presumably.

BH: Yes, those things. Of course, staging and musical things but, for example, if I decided to sing the high C or the high D in the Lulu scene with a particular color one night, I won't attempt to repeat that every night. I don't even think about it, because in performance I'm in a state of almost improvisation. When you know the score so well and when you're so inside the piece, to me when it's really good, it feels like an improvisation.

NG: Right. You're creating it?

BH: Like you're a co-creator.

NG: How about when you're doing an opera you've done before, but with a new director? Do you entirely start over?

BH: That doesn't happen very often. I've only done that with only *Pelléas et Mélisande* and *Lulu*.

I wouldn't do a second production of an opera with a different director unless I really, really wanted to work with that director. With Katie Mitchell and with Warlikowski for the *Mélisande*, I knew they would be just polar opposites. Then, with Marthaler and Warlikowski for the *Lulu*. I also, I had such high respect for Marthaler, that even though I loved the Warlikowski production that we had done, I was really, really curious what Marthaler would do with it.

NG: Was it difficult to start with a clean slate again after you had already done a production?

BH: No, it wasn't difficult at all. No. No, but I know the other production, like *Written On Skin*, I don't want to do any more productions of that. I felt that what we did with Katie Mitchell was extremely fulfilling and I would never do another staging of it and with *Die Soldaten*, that I did with [Andres] Kriegeburg: same thing. That was maybe the most perfect production that I feel I've ever been involved in, and I wouldn't go and sing it in another production.

NG: Wow. Okay. Well, that's a real luxury that you can make that choice, but unfortunately for the audiences who would love to see you perform these roles, that's disappointing. Hopefully they're available on video at least.

BH: Yes. Most of them are.

NG: As far as your decisions about the expressive content inherent in the score, does that come as you start studying it or does that evolve through the rehearsal process?

BH: Both. It comes immediately, even before I start singing the score, when I'm just looking at it, it starts to come in. I'll be constantly making associations, like musical associations, technical associations, perhaps in the passaggio area, or how I might negotiate areas where I need to use a mix with chest voice or whatever. Also, associations with film characters, or with a color, or with another piece that I sang. I think, "Oh yeah, I'm going to maybe associate this with that moment in that piece." I'll write them all in the score. When I work, I never work purely technically. It's everything all the time. Then, as I continue the rehearsal process, usually what happens with me is that I go too far in staging physically.

I usually get to a point where I'm not singing very well in the rehearsals, which is fine, because I'm used to that. I go through that, because I want to get to the boundary of the theatrical aspect. Then, once I've reached where I want to be dramatically, then the actor in me makes a deal with the singer that we're now going to let the singer's body do what it needs to do as well. Then I come back. I think other people go the other way: They want to have it always, always, always perfect in the voice. They limit the staging at all times whereas, I will go very far in the staging. Then, I will bring the staging back to the—

NG: You'll see how far you can go without compromising your vocal production.

BH: Totally. Usually for me, I find new colors and new approaches by pushing my theatrical limits.

NG: I see. It sounds like, as you're learning the music to begin with, you're open to your spirit of inquiry, but at a certain point you sort of cut it off. You just make note of possibilities, so that you can draw on them later after you're working with your director and conductor. Is that correct?

BH: Yeah. I don't make any decisions. I just keep everything open and I'm the kind of person that goes into a rehearsal and presents a lot of options. I don't sing it square blank, but I'm flexible, extremely flexible. Even if we're in the first rehearsal with piano, if we repeat something, I'll do it differently. I'll never do it the same, because I don't want to get stuck in anything.

NG: Right and you also want your conductor, primarily your conductor, to see that you've got lots of possibilities.

BH: To be honest, it's more the director. If it was a luxury situation when the conductor's there all the time, that's great, but that's quite rare. Only with Petrenko and Jurowski and George Benjamin did I have conductors who were present for the entire rehearsal period of a production. In other words, the conductor's not there. I generally have an assistant who's conducting and who doesn't have any—

NG: —say, ultimately.

BH: Right. My presentation of things is more for the director and then, but in the case of Vlad [Vladimir Jurowski], or [Kiril] Petrenko, then it's a different story, because they're present, as a conductor should be.

NG: Right. Well, that's an alarming state of affairs. I can't imagine doing a production and leaving in the middle of it and coming back, but—

BH: Yeah, but that's how most opera productions are. The conductor is usually there first couple of days and they'd leave and then they come back once the staging is done. It's really a big issue that I have with the opera business now, because I don't understand how we can really make a work as a team. Imagine if the director left.

NG: Yeah, it's hard to develop a real musical and artistic *esprit de corps*. I get that.

BH: Exactly. Yeah.

NG: I have another important question, which is, do you approach song repertoire the same way, when you don't have a conductor or director?

BH: Yeah. I think maybe the ratios end up being a little bit different because there's a lot more *Barbara* in the song repertoire in a recital program and there's a lot more of *whatever character I'm playing* in the opera when I'm in an opera production, but I'm still looking for the subtext all the time. The subtext is the real story. That storytelling in the recital song repertoire is extremely important to me. I hold it. I don't do that many recitals. When I do, I hold a certain energy for the entire thing. It's a complete work. Whether it's eighty minutes or sixty minutes, it's like one entire event: There's a through line for that whole event.

NG: When you're rehearsing with either your pianist or your chamber ensemble, do you actually include them in on the discussions about what the goals might be? Musical goals are?

BH: No, I don't talk about it and I don't find it necessary because in a way, I don't even want to define it. I just know that it will be there and that there's a certain spirit or energy that is there.

NG: They'll either click in or they won't?

BH: Yes. They'll get it or they don't, but it doesn't matter because I am so lucky that I get to work basically only with musicians that I really want to work with.

NG: I'd like to know how you get into a spirit of performance psychologically.

BH: Yeah. There is a certain physicality that ... Oh. Well, one thing that's interesting is that I steal from every show. I always put a little bit of another show in the new show and I do it on purpose. It's like an homage. I never tell what it is, but I'll steal a gesture from a dance production I did with Sasha Waltz and put it in *Die Soldaten*. I'll take a gesture from *Die Soldaten* and I'll put it in *Pelléas et Mélisande* and I'll take something from *Pelléas et Mélisande* and I'll put it in the next opera.

NG: It sounds like, in a production a new gesture might widen your artistic vocabulary, and then you inject that into other characters. Then, you just make note of where they're from.

BH: Well, no. It's like a composer quoting another composer or quoting himself. It's a humorous thing, but it's not just humorous. It's also a reminder of the trajectory of the career and the life. That's because in a way, I was a co-creator, let's say. In the staging things that I do, someone came up to me the other day and they said, "Oh, I've thought what the movement coach taught you to do in Katie Mitchell's *Pelléas et Mélisande*." I said, "What movement coach?" She said, "Oh, wasn't there a guy who taught movement." I do this really extreme shoulder roll where I balance on my shoulder and my feet are in the air and it was spectacular. I said, "Oh, it didn't have anything to do with him."

And she said, "Oh, I thought he choreographed that." I was like, "No." I offer a lot. I remember one day in rehearsal when I was lying on the floor at the end of a particular scene and Katie Mitchell said, "Can you find an interesting way to get up to standing?" I said, "Okay, sure." She went off and worked with someone else. Half an hour later she came back to me and I had figured out this crazy slow motion shoulder roll. That was it, but I'll come, and I'll offer a lot of physical possibilities.

I offer a lot and I made sure that I don't repeat things. With the directors, we're working in a really, really febrile kind of intensity. This way is very important for me because I think some performers like to be told where to go and what to do, whereas other performers offer a lot. I know I offer a lot. I don't like to be told where to go and what to do. I like to just collaborate. I remember with Christoph Marthaler, whenever we got really tired, I would just go up to him and I would kind of punch him in the shoulder and teasingly say, "Why can't you just tell me where to go and what to do?" It was nice because that's kind of how he knew I didn't want that.

16

Audra McDonald

Audra McDonald (b. 1970) is the leading musical-theater performer today. A six-time Tony Award winner, she trained as a voice major at the Juilliard School. She has performed in opera, musical-theater, plays with no music, concerts, films, and in recurring roles on television. McDonald has done it all, and she brings sincerity, emotional conviction, and professionalism to everything she undertakes.

Neal Goren: I would like to ask you a few questions. Actually, we'll start with one, and we'll see where it takes us. Because this book is about process and artistic self-empowerment for singers, I'm interviewing a few people like yourself about their process. So I wanted to ask you, when you embark upon learning a new role or one you're unfamiliar with, do you start with the text or the music?

Audra McDonald: Well, you know, I may have, for many reasons, a very different answer than some of the other people you're interviewing, because a lot of times I'm playing characters that speak quite a bit.

NG: I welcome divergent points of view.

AM: For me, I start with the text.

NG: Well, actually all of the great artists I've interviewed thus far have said that they start with the text in order to form their character.

AM: Because if you think about it, in most cases, a lot of times maybe the composers were starting with the texts too.

NG: Certainly.

AM: The text is going to help begin to unravel the mystery of who this character is, and what their wants and needs and desires are. You can find that not only by what they say and what they proclaim, but what other people say about them, and the situation that they're in. I absolutely head to the text first. That's where your first clues lie.

NG: When you embark on this, do you embark with a spirit of inquiry as you're reading the text?

AM: Oh, absolutely. Yes. I do a lot of Q&A sessions and master classes with students. I always tell them that your work as a student never ends when you go into performing, especially when you're taking on roles, or even just singing songs like I do for concerts. It's still about knowing what, excavating the soul of the character that you are inhabiting to either sing the song or to play the role or to sing the whatever it is. You have to excavate all that is there. So everything is a research paper.

Once you excavate the soul of who the character is, then it's like, okay, so what was life like at the time that this play or this song takes place, or whatever, you know? So yes, it's constant inquiry, and then finding all that resonates within yourself.

NG: Then after you've looked at the text like that, what you just alluded to is then you start researching the context. Is that true?

AM: Yes, absolutely. You know, Billie Holiday, doing the Lady Day, I was able to read the text of what Lanie Robinson wrote in his play, but then I had to research everything there was to research about Billie Holiday, and listen to every snippet of audio recording and video recording, anything that I could find, and read every book I could find about her, and every interview, not only by her, but about her and people who knew her. Then I tried to meet as many people that knew her. All of it to try and bring her to life for myself, and then discover who all that was within me. So yeah, it's like being a detective or an archeologist.

NG: The question is, isn't it a different sort of procedure for a bio play like that than it might be for something else that's more of a narrative?

AM: I wouldn't say so.

NG: No?

AM: Porgy and Bess was the same thing. I went down to South Carolina. I went and saw where Catfish Row was based upon, what DuBose Heyward had in mind. I read DuBose Heyward's books. I studied life for, not only African Americans at the time, but African American women, what their choices were, what they could and couldn't do. I researched my own family, all of it. No, I don't find any of it different at all.

Frankie and Johnny, I just performed. There's no music in that, but I was researching PTSD. I was researching victims of domestic violence, as well as researching what it's like to be a waitress and work at a diner, and New York in the 80s, all of it. It's all research.

NG: When you then get into the music, how do you transfer what you've learned from the text and the research into the music, or do you just ask questions about the music as you go along?

AM: No. I don't see it as a transfer. I may ask questions and try to understand what the composer meant, or if it's not completely explicit, or isn't something that I completely understand, I'll try and study it to see why the composer goes up at this point, or why this is pianissimo. But I am a firm believer in what Terrence McNally wrote for Maria Callas to say in the play Master Class, that the composer is God, that the composer has done the work for you in that sense. So I then use that as another map as well.

That also gives me more information about the character, because the composer's a part of that creative process.

NG: Right.

AM: It's my job to interpret all of that and bring it to life, so in that sense, it's, once again, studying and researching and understanding what the composer has laid out.

NG: Do you sometimes analyze for yourself what the expressive content of the music is and how it relates to what you want to communicate?

AM: Absolutely. Absolutely. Why am I falling? Why is the pitch descending here? What does that signify to the composer, and what did the composer want to signify about what's happening in that moment? You can hear something going on in certain songs, you can hear the heartbeat happening in the accompaniment. Why is that happening? What's happening to the character in that moment? Once again, it's all clues, not even clues, it's just, it's all part of telling the story.

NG: What strikes me as being a constant for you, is the spirit of inquiry both as you approach the text and then when you go into the music.

AM: Absolutely.

NG: I think part of it is that one has to actually love feeling like a student that way.

AM: I hated being a student, but I love discovering characters, and I love inhabiting characters, inhabiting roles and performance. That is part of it for me. I love that discovery.

NG: So you like being the detective or the archeologist, as you said.

AM: Yes, yes. I love that. That thrills me. A lot of people, especially in music theater, say the rehearsal is the best part, when you're doing all that excavating and discovering and figuring it out. Especially for us Broadway folks, because once you've figured it all out, and you start doing it on a nightly basis, you can still discover stuff. But then it becomes about how to keep it alive night after night after night after night after night for a year or two.

NG: Was it the same when you sang Bess?

AM: What do you mean?

NG: That you kept on discovering as you went along?

AM: Absolutely. I was making, based on what I knew about her and what I knew that DuBose Heyward had written about her, and what George Gershwin and Ira Gershwin had discovered about the story and the people, I was still giving myself little ideas and thoughts about what could be going on in her mind all the way up until the end. I won't even go into what I had, thoughts I had about Bess and her actual relationship to certain people in Catfish Row toward the end, but it gave me fodder for why Bess was so attached to Clara's baby at the end.

Yeah. Constant discovery.

NG: That's beautiful. I remember I was, oddly enough, though I'm a pianist, I was a student of Jacqueline du Pre, the cellist.

AM: Oh, wow.

NG: Yeah, it was great. We spent a lot of time always discussing what the emotional content was of any phrase of any piece, and what it is we wanted to communicate and where, because she said only if you have a clear idea of what you want to communicate, can you communicate it, otherwise you're sure to fail.

AM: Right, exactly.

NG: So in order for you develop your concept of the character, you begin the minute you start looking at the text, and then your concept continues evolving over time with the research, and then as you study the music and inquire about that, and then it keeps on going on through performances. Is that correct?

AM: Absolutely, because it has to stay alive. We're live performers. Every night it has to be there, because maybe it's your ninety-ninth time doing it, and believe me, I've done shows that I've done one hundred, two hundred performances of something, but it's the audience's first time, so it's got to be like the first time for them. The present, the now, the discovery needs to be there.

NG: With each performance, you relive it, essentially.

AM: You have to.

Diane Soviero

Diana Soviero (b. 1946) is known as one of the greatest interpreters of Italian lyric and *lirico-spinto* soprano roles of her generation. She sang extensively at the Metropolitan Opera, New York City Opera, and internationally and was particularly celebrated for her interpretation of Puccini's *Suor Angelica* and Verdi's *La Traviata*, as well as dozens of others. She stood out among her contemporaries for her excellence as a singing actor. Presently on the voice faculty of the Mannes College of Music, she passes her knowledge on to the next generation of singing actors.

Neal Goren: I want to learn about your process: When you were setting out to learn an unfamiliar role, did you start with the text or with the music?

Diana Soviero: With the text. I wanted to see what was going on with the text. I wanted to see who I was going to portray, and then right away, I went into the orchestra score. We were—

NG: Right away?

DS: —right away. And my teachers always taught us, at the Julliard prep, that we had to know every instrument that was accompanying us and what was going on. In case there was a problem in the orchestra, we had to know what happened. So as I said before, our teachers used to tell us to use the orchestra score to see which instruments were accompanying us. Was it the horns, was it the celli, was it viola? Who was in that forte with us? Why was it there? If there was an oboe in my passaggio, I was a little concerned because it would be blasting in my passaggio and I'd go, "Oi, oi, oi!" You know, and all these things we were taught: how to study; for two and a half years at—I was thirteen through sixteen—at the prep school.

NG: What I want to know is how you would develop your characters. So you would start with the text.

DS: Yeah, I'd look and see it. In fact, that's how I learned Pagliacci. I was with my pianist . . . This is a very interesting story. I was at Juilliard, and very young—seventeen, eighteen not even—and I said to my pianist, I want to go to the library. Come with me because I want to take some scores out, and let's go over some different operas that we don't know about. And let's see what we're going to do in a few . . . You know, we were very crazy.

DS: And he's looking through the music and he says, "Oh my God, look at this. Man-on le-Scott," and I said, "No, it's Manon Les-co," and blah, blah, blah. And he goes, "Oh my God, Pagalakey." And I go, "Let me look at . . . 'Pagliacci.'" Let's look at this . . . Hmm . . . and he starts playing the stuff and, and go, "Oh!" I said, "Jareth, oh my gosh! I have a whip, and I have the this . . . And then this. And then there's a Commedia and I have to change my character. Oh my God, this is amazing! Oh my God. Oh my God."

Before long, my teacher said to me, "You know, there's an audition for some group. You should go sing . . . blah, blah, blah." And I was auditioning for Kurt Herbert Adler. I was very green.

NG: Whoa!

DS: Wait! And I told him the list and he was, "Oh!" he said. "Soprano, lyric soprano." And I said, "Yes, maestro, I sing Donde Lieta." "Do you have anything coloratura?" And I said, "I have Traviata, but I'm just learning it. It's new." So, I went home, and I told my mother, and I was very sad, and she said, "What's the matter?" I said, "Mom, I don't know. I had an audition today. And the conductor said to me he knew exactly what I was doing, and I felt, I don't know, I guess I wasn't really special or something . . ." And she didn't answer me right away. I was helping her wash the dishes because that's what you did. "Why don't you find something none of your friends can do, and maybe you'll be different. Because you know, DS, you're very special."

I said, "Oh, Mom, you're so good! That's because you're my mom . . . and blah, blah, blah."

I had the score of Pagliacci. NG, I studied the score, and it was the first opera I sang in every major opera house in the world.

NG: Indeed. So, after you learned the text, or at least studied it—

DS: Learn the text. Learn the music.

NG: Was there a level of inquiry that you brought to these—

DS: Definitely. I watched the movie. Oh God, I can't even remember its title.

NG: La Strada?

DS: La Strada. I did a lot of research about the Commedia. I got all the books in the library about the Commedia. I still have them here.

And I wanted to know what it was about. And being Sicilian . . . My family was Sicilian. I could go into that with Cavalleria and Pagliacci very easily because of my background. So, it was easy for me to say, "Aspide, va! Ti sei svelato ormai!" You know, like stuff like that. And it was easy for me to do that.

Now, I found letters that I had written to myself as Manon. (This is going back way . . . years, way years, for years.) "DS, where were you coming from? Why are you alone? Do you have a family? What did you do that you're going to the convent, DS? When you're in the coach, how far is it from where you're coming from to where . . . to the port? Do you have anything with you? Do you have any luggage with you? Do you have anything to eat with you as you get off the coach? Are you perspired? Were you flirted with? Were you annoyed? Were you nauseous?" I did all this, and when I did my first rehearsal, I said to . . . I don't even remember who the director was . . . "Can I have an apple in my basket?" And he looked at me and he says, "What's the matter? Didn't you have lunch?" You know, like he was making a joke. I said, "No, because when I come out, I want to have a handkerchief. I want to take my hat off because there's a fountain. Can we have water in there?" He says, "What are you talking about? There's no faucet." I says, "But can you put a pail of water in there? So, I can go in there and go, 'Ah!' because—"

NG: Because you've been traveling for how many hours? And . . .

DS: And then I took the apple and when des Grieux comes down the steps, before he says . . . introduces himself, and I, with the apple, I go . . . And I had the apple in my mouth. I threw it in the basket. I wiped my mouth, and I sat there. And it was the beginning of my life as an actress. This, I took that with me at a very young age.

NG: So did you also look at the score and say, "I've got enough time to do this"?

DS: Yes. The composer wrote it for me. Because I had all this interval music in between and I said, "What am I going to do now? What am I thinking?" What am I looking at? Why am I there? Am I nervous? Am I meeting somebody? Yes, I am. Do I know who he is? Have I seen a photo of him? No. I mean, how do I know? So, I'm looking at everybody. Who is he? Who is he, really?

So, all these things I developed and then, of course, as I grew up in the business and got better, a little bit better . . . Then after that, forty years ago, I met Bernard [Uzan], who changed my life because Beverly [Sills] called me into her office and she said, "Okay, sit down. Who are you working with?"

And I said. "What are you talking about?" She says, "What's changed you?" And I said, "Well, I met this French guy, and he's a director. And he's been helping me." She said, "Well, whatever it is, don't stop." And then we got married. Interesting, right . . . And I remember my first Butterfly. I said, "I have to know about what the life of the geisha is." And then my coach said, "But it's not about a Japanese girl. It's about the tune, this Italian music, DS. You will have to know that it's very visceral. It's very . . . Japanese women are very much like this." So, I said, "You mean I have to separate myself? Like do less physical things and more vocal things?" And when I was offered the job to do the Bob Wilson production, I at first didn't want to do it. And Bernard said to me, "You sit down. You're doing it." And I said, "But, Bernard, I can't do my shtick." He said, "Imagine, DS, what you can do not moving, what you can do with your voice. It'll change the opera world." And I said, "You know what? That's a challenge. I'm going to take it." Because I called my agent and I said, "I'm accepting the job." "You are?" They were shocked. "You are?" And Bob was over the top when he knew I was doing it. But I was . . .

NG: —frightened? Were you concerned that if you weren't able to do your thing—

DS: Yes, very much. I was nervous because I wanted it to be perfect.

NG: Right. And you couldn't do what you relied on, what you thought was your strength.

DS: Exactly. So, I was nervous

NG: So, when you were developing your character ideas, did you consult the score as you were doing it?

DS: Oh my God, yes!

NG: Okay. So that actually brings me to another question.

DS: Good!

NG: When you sang non-Italian repertoire, did you approach it exactly the same way?

DS: Definitely. It was my language. I didn't have to worry about it.

The thing that I had to worry about was . . . I had to be, I think more . . . I would say more specific in the text because if it were in English . . . At City Opera, we did everything in English, and I remember Julius Rudel saying that he didn't want to have to go, "What?" when we were singing. Everything had to be perfectly, clearly enunciated.

NG: So, the priority was communication?

DS: Exactly.

NG: So, communication, not just of the words but of the characters.

DS: Everything. Body language. Everything important. If my character was upset, how would I show it? What would my demeanor be? Would I walk out like that if I was upset? No. There would be something I would be worried about. So I would have to . . . My concentration wouldn't be right. I'd be looking around; I would be searching, or something.

And in a more dramatic role . . . I know that one production of . . . I think it was Traviata that Bernard was directing me. He said, "DS, you're all over the place here. What are you doing?" And I said, "Well, I'm acting." He said, "Don't act." He said, "Stop for a moment. Stay still, DS. Use the power you have in your throat to tell me how you're feeling. And if you have to cry, cry. I don't care. Sing through your tears." Whoa! The idea of the *Passato* at the end of Traviata, the tears coming down my face, and I said, "I have to stop. I have to do something." He said, "No, keep going." But if I didn't feel it, I can't make them feel it. I had to do it myself first, and then I would be able to convince my audience that I knew what I was doing. And tell them what I feel as if I didn't know. I can't tell anybody how I feel.

NG: So, were your intentions generalized, or were they specific, or both?

DS: I would say both. Maybe I could say both. Because there's always a mixture.

NG: There's got to be some freedom in performance.

DS: Exactly. There has to be something all of a sudden that I would think, "Oh, I can do that with that word." Maybe it means that . . . Boom! Let me go back and see. Is that the music of somebody in the opera that I'm hearing in my subconscious, before I say the word? What's happening here? Is it bringing me into another place that I have to think about? Hmm. Let me think about that for a moment.

How do I feel about that? Can I take that from inside my soul?

NG: So, you were very clear in your mind what you wanted to convey.

DS: Exactly.

NG: What the composer wanted you to communicate.

DS: Yes. In the beginning of my career, the directors and conductors didn't know that I had such an inquisitive mind. So they would tell me what they wanted. Then it was up to me to see if I could do what they wanted and be convincing . . . I should say, be able to digest what they wanted. And if the director was—how do I say—believing in me as an actress, they'd say, "Great, let me see that." Right. Let me see that.

NG: So they were willing to collaborate.

DS: Yes. Some were not, and they kept me in a cage: "Don't do this. Don't move. Don't do that. Right there. Don't do that." You know? Sometimes I had to deal with that, but I was very professional about it. I never argued with them. I tried so hard to do

...Even the conductor...Tried so hard to do what they wanted. Even if it was a different tempo and my voice couldn't maybe go that fast at that time. I needed to take a breath, or whatever. I had to adjust. And this is what I teach the kids, too. You have to adjust.

NG: So did you try and find, how can I say, emotional ways within yourself to justify what they were asking for?

DS: I had to develop a vivid imagination. I had a fabulous life. There were no crises in my life. I was never abused. I was never killed.

NG: So you were empathic.

DS: Yes, I, I was easily . . . a sponge.

NG: So, when you would work with different directors, or if you were repeating a role you hadn't done for a number of years but with a different director, did you start the process . . . Did you look at the score—

DS: All over. In fact, I had about twelve different Traviata scores. I have a few scores of all different conductors that worked with me, and markings of all different conductors that I used when I was working.

NG: So when you were working with your conductors and your directors, it sounds like you somehow—because of your personal skills and your personality—you were able to develop a collaborative relationship—

DS: Very much so. Very much so. Are you kidding? I've seen conductors bury people. And that could easily be done. Very easily. They have the power. They have the power. And my way—

NG: So you gained their respect.

DS: —now that I'm not with conductors all the time, I can tell you my secret.

NG: Please!

DS: If I knew that there was a difficult passage in whatever ...
Othello, whatever I was saying, I would, in the interval, at intermission, I would ask the conductor, "Maestro, I need your help."
"DS, what's the matter?" "Maestro, in this measure here, right
here, the bar? I need here ... because look what's happening here
in the orchestra, blah, blah, blah, blah, blah. I need your help
because I have to build this phrase and I want to make it so gor-
geous on that arch. I need your help. How are we going to do it
together?"

    I talked to him like an instrumentalist. And then when I was
up on stage, in the first orchestra rehearsal, he'd look at me like,
"Is that okay?" And I'd go [she gives a thumbs-up] You know, so
there was this kind of, first of all, respect—

NG: Respect and trust.

DS: Trust. And I knew what was going on in the orchestra.

NG: Did you figure these things out yourself or were you taught?

DS: No, I had the training. Yeah. And then of course, being a nut
and inquisitive, I learned by myself.

Christa Ludwig

Christa Ludwig (b. 1928) is a legendary Austrian mezzo soprano, known equally for her singing of opera and *Lieder*. Her operatic repertoire was incredibly broad, even extending to some roles normally sung by sopranos.

In the following interview, it is clear that her artistic concerns were often principally practical. I include it virtually uncut because she discusses subjects as far-ranging as artistic flexibility and collaboration, professionalism, learning atonal music, and how her approach to learning opera roles differed from her approach to learning *Lieder*.

Christa Ludwig: Mahler said that interpretation is not written in the notes. And I mean, this is so essential, really essential, because while I learned Mahler phrasing from Karajan and also from my mother, of course; but from Bernstein I learned about the true spirit of the music.

Neal Goren: What I've noticed from listening to many, many, many recordings, is that *Lieder* was very different before Schwarzkopf than after Schwarzkopf. Earlier, there had been great freedom in *Lieder* singing.

CL: And then came Fischer-Dieskau and Schwarzkopf.

NG: Exactly. And everything changed. It became, how shall I say, much more rigid and "correct." But it didn't have the same sort of spontaneity.

CL: But this was Walter Legge.

NG: That's what I have been told.

CL: He was the man who said, "It's like this and like this and like this and like this." I learned with him also a lot about *Lieder* singing. Of course, I'm grateful, but it was a time where everything had to be in the right key and you shouldn't breathe here, you shouldn't breathe there, and everything was Schwarzkopf/Fischer-Dieskau, *ja*.

NG: So interpretation was micromanaged.

CL: *Ja, ja*. It was too much. It was too much.

NG: And it lost the verve.

CL: *Ja. Ja*, of course. And because Schwarzkopf sang a lot for records, and you don't see the face, the expression. So when making the records, she made the whole expression with her voice. When she was singing *Lieder* in Germany, we understood the words. Even though she did not need to explain the words here [this interview took place in Vienna], she did anyway. So her interpretation was always too much.

NG: Right. It always seemed like she explained the individual words but not the phrase.

CL: *Ja*, no the words. Every word. Every word.

NG: Or not the song, the individual words. Exactly.

CL: Every single word.

NG: *Ja*. So, not quite to my taste, but she changed things very drastically.

CL: She was a great artist. It's also the highest level.

NG: No question.

CL: And I criticize . . .

NG: I understand. But comparing her *Lieder* interpretation to what came before: Elisabeth Schumann, and all the recordings with Strauss playing for people, there had been a freedom that was . . .

CL: But I didn't hear Schumann, also. I sang *Lieder* before, but I learned it in Vienna with Schwarzkopf and Siegfried, and Prey and Fischer-Dieskau. So, this was my generation where I learned.

NG: I played a concert for Prey many years ago.

CL: Oh, *ja?* He sang always a little bit flat.

NG: He was a delight. Yes, but he was such a . . .

CL: The voice was very beautiful.

NG: Beautiful. And a beautiful personality, too.

NG: Can we start what I wanted to ask you specifically—

CL: *Ja, ja.* Ask me.

NG: Which is, when you went and started to learn a new role that you actually didn't know at all, or had not been acquainted with, where did you begin? Did you begin with the music? Did you begin with the text? How did you develop your character?

CL: So, I tell you a story.

NG: Please.

CL: My mother read in the newspaper Karajan is doing *Parsifal.* She said to me, CL, you must sing Kundry. I had never seen *Parsifal,* I didn't know Kundry: I had no idea. So, I went to Karajan and said, "My mother said . . ." Because the two of them, they worked together thirty years prior in Aachen. They sang together *Fidelio, Frau ohne Schatten,* and everything, and I said to Karajan, "My mother said I should sing Kundry." "Well, did you sing it before?" I said, "No." "How can you dare to think that you could sing it?"

NG: Were you very young, or were you already an experienced singer?

CL: It was the sixties. It was a good time. The end of my thirtieth years, forty years . . .

NG: You were already a very experienced singer and you had worked with him, too.

CL: *Ja.* So I said, "You know, with you, I could sing it." And I sang it. Of course, I first look, where is the highest note and where is the lowest note? Then I had a look through the tessitura because I can sing this high note [she demonstrates], but singing a scale up, it is impossible. This is the first thing I had a look. In the opera, mostly, the text I don't mind, mostly. Not when Hofmannstahl made the text. This is wonderful.

NG: But Kundry is a very complicated character to understand.

CL: Wonderful. Because her character changes on stage. So I loved it. I loved a lot. Kundry changes and *Frau ohne Schatten*, the Frau, she changes, too.

NG: Did you ever sing the Amme, also?

CL: No. Never, I couldn't. It was too dramatic. I was not on the dramatic side. I was on the lyric side. I had a small-scaled voice.

NG: But it carried very well in the theater.

CL: It carried. *Ja*, because of overtones.

NG: Squillo.

CL: Unlike opera, the first thing with *Lieder*, it is the poem which interests me. So, this is the reason I don't like so many Schubert songs. I don't like them! Once I was asked to record all the female Schubert songs. I didn't. I did two records or whatever, but not more, because I think they are terrible.

NG: Right, so in operatic repertoire, you looked and saw if it was appropriate for your voice, and then you went to the text?

CL: No. The music. The music, for me, is more important than the text in opera.

NG: If you're not analyzing the text, how do you figure out who the character is? Who Kundry is?

CL: No, I read the book by [Houston Stewart] Chamberlain.

NG: You read a book by Chamberlain?

CL: *Ja*, because he thinks that Kundry ... the opera is very dangerous. Kundry is a Jewish lady. Klingsor makes the ... [she mimes self-castration]. Before this was kissed by the Jewess. This is the *blessure* ...

NG: The wound.

CL: The wound which could never heal. And only because Kundry is dying at the end, she is saved. So, I read this book and I think, "This is Kundry." So, I come from the other side.

NG: That was enough? Did you agree with the book after you had performed it?

CL: I did. I did.

NG: How about when you sang new music?

CL: I did a lot of new music. New music is completely different. I learned I don't have an absolute ear. I had a coach in the opera. He made on the piano a normal accompaniment. With normal tonic. Tonal?

NG: So, he made a tonal arrangement of the accompaniment for you to learn.

CL: Then I could learn it easily. Then I knew it, and he could play something underneath me and I sang with it.

NG: Could you still sing the correct pitches when his arrangement was replaced by the real accompaniment?

CL: By then, he could play whatever he wanted.

NG: Once you had it in your voice.

CL: I had it in my voice.

NG: I see. And did you concern yourself with the character, also, in these new pieces? Or was it just more about singing it?

CL: One role I loved to sing, but this was not entirely atonal: "The Visit."

NG: Yes, von Einem.

CL: Von Einem. Even though it was not entirely atonal, I never learned it right because I had no time. But I was good in the expression, and I loved the role, the story was fantastic, but I never really learned it. Nobody heard it correctly!

NG: I see. But the story . . .

CL: Fantastic.

NG: You understood . . .

CL: *Ja*, the other stories in opera are mostly the same. I don't care about opera: I never go! Yes, I go to *Götterdämmerung*, to *Frau ohne Schatten*, to *Wozzeck*, sometimes to *Pelléas et Mélisande*, but I cannot listen anymore to oom-pah-pah.

NG: You're not interested in early Verdi anymore or . . .

CL: Oh no, I cannot bear it anymore.

NG: But you sang some of those.

CL: Yes, but you know since when I was four years old, I'm fed up with classical music and singing opera. Both parents were opera singers and they had a school and I heard when the students were singing all the time. I had enough of Verdi.

NG: You sang Eboli: That was one of your great roles.

CL: Eboli's a funny role. When I was very young, I was twenty-four, I sang Eboli for the very first time in Darmstadt.

NG: At twenty-four? Wow. Okay.

CL: The very first aria was "The Veil," I sang beautifully. And the second aria, the dramatic aria . . .

NG: *O don fatale.*

CL: I couldn't sing very well. Then came the time where I could sing both arias good. And then came the time when the first aria with the coloratura went not so good, but the other one, the dramatic. Then came the time where I could nothing anymore! The aria ["O don fatale"] is very difficult. I had a very bad time once in Salzburg Festival. I couldn't sing it; not good. And I had a divorce, I had a new love, I had my menopause, and I was a mess. And so, it wasn't terrible, but it didn't go well. I was with Karajan, and he was *very* slow.

NG: Did you ever sing with Leontyne Price?

CL: Of course. I sang with her a lot of Verdi *Requiem.* I sang *Aida* with her. She was the best. This was my black *orchidée.*

NG: Black Orchid.

CL: Orchid, *ja:* my black orchid. When she sang for the very last time in Vienna, I really was angry that I wouldn't hear anymore this smoky voice. I was angry. I was furious that she sang for the last time. I loved her voice. I loved this. Then suddenly not to hear this voice anymore, this was terrible.

NG: I loved playing for her. It was one of the greatest experiences of my life. Each performance was different, and she listened so acutely when I was at the keyboard. She listened to everything I did and would respond musically. Then I would react to her. You know what it's like to give a great concert . . .

CL: Of course it is necessary. It has to be like this. I had once an accompanist. This was Irwin Gage, very good, but it was impossible with the two of us. He played his Schubert, and I sang my Schubert. Was impossible.

NG: And was that just because he was not flexible, or he wasn't listening?

CL: No, he wasn't flexible . . .

NG: Or was it his personality?

CL: Both. Not flexible and personality. It was impossible. When we had an arrangement to come together at 4:30 or whatever, he came at 5:00. There are things I don't like very much. So, I'm too Prussian.

NG: Did you work with my teacher, Geoffrey Parsons?

CL: Of course. Wonderful. I liked him more than the other famous one.

NG: Gerald Moore?

CL: *Ja*, because Moore was too British for me. He was playing with beautiful sound, but personally, I like more flexible.

NG: Every singer has his priorities. The first time I played for Leontyne, she said, "Maestro, I do not want an accompanist: I want a partner. I want to feel like I'm surrounded by sound all the time. I don't want to be cushioned, I want to be surrounded." And she had a big voice. A lyric voice, but a voice like yours that cut.

CL: Of course, it is necessary because, also, I say always to my conductors, "Give me a carpet. I need a carpet."

NG: And then you can fly together.

CL: *Ja*. On the carpet, *ja*.

NG: So, I want to go back to developing characters. How about when you did a role for the twentieth time with a new stage director and they had different ideas?

CL: I don't know. I was lucky in my life. I had, always, very good conductors and very good stage directors.

NG: Did they ever move you in a different direction than you had expected with the music or the character?

CL: No, we could speak about the character. For example, I am the anti-type of Carmen. I had two, three times Carmen in Germany and it was not good. So I was not the type of Carmen. And then here in Vienna, again, Carmen. The first time I was the substitute for Maderna. Is this the name?

NG: The conductor Bruno Maderna?

CL: No, not him. A singer: Jane Madeira. Forgotten, *ja*. She was a wonderful-looking woman with a dark voice, sexy voice. She was really very good. American Carmen, but very good. I was the second Carmen, and this was a flop. Then came again, Carmen. And this was with Otto Schenk, the stage director. I went first to him and said, "You know, I had so bad experiences with my Carmen. Tell me, how do you see Carmen? If it is with a rose here and a fan here, then that's not me." No, he said, "It is a woman from next door. She is a free character. She is free. She is normal woman. She made free love and she doesn't care about nothing." This I could do. So, I would go to the stage director and ask, "How do you see this role?" And then I could do it. But ask!

I spoke also, always, with my conductor. I said to Bernstein, when it was a little too quick, I said, "Lenny, I cannot sing like this." Or when it was Böhm in Tristan und Isolde when it was too slow, I said "I have no breath anymore: I cannot sing it. Do it a little bit, a little bit quicker." "CL, then it is a waltz." But he did it.

NG: And he did it to accommodate you?

CL: Of course. And Karajan, when we made Missa Solemnis, Gundula Janowitz came to me and said, "CL, I cannot sing the Benedictus. This is too slow. Too slow. I cannot sing it anymore." I said, "Speak with him." "No, no, no: You speak with him." I was always the one. I went to him, "Karajan, the Benedictus is much too slow to sing." "Then I have to look for other singers." I said: "Better than us, you won't get."

And he did it a little bit quicker. I always spoke with my conductors. "Here, help me please." I learned this from Hermann Scherchen. He said advised me to say, "Please help me." And this "help me" was always in my ear. I went to my conductors and said, "Please, you have to help me. I cannot sing this. I have to breathe here. And this, a little bit there." And then they did it.

NG: The byproduct, or "please help me," is that you develop a sense of partnership with them.

CL: *Ja*, of course. I had once a conductor who came from Czechoslovakia, and for me, I couldn't sing with this man. It was impossible. And from my own money I canceled eight performances. I couldn't sing with him. No, I couldn't.

NG: I see. So part of having a successful career is knowing what you can do well, and making a partnership with your conductor and your director.

CL: Of course.

NG: Did you ever have a conductor with ideas that were contrary to yours?

CL: No. My three famous conductors were Böhm, Bernstein, and Karajan. They were the three. Then also it's Klemperer, then it's Solti, Barenboim in Vienna, and Mehta, of course. They were all very good conductors. It was normal.

NG: Did you work with Kleiber also?

CL: Once. We did a concert here. Very good. It was broadcast on the radio. We didn't get paid: nothing, nothing. I got a little CD. I don't know where it is: Chaos! He was very good. But he was different. And he wanted the last song of Das Lied von der Erde everything piano. This was for the audience and for the critic not good. One has to sing it, and he wanted this already in the other realm.

NG: How about stage directors? Were there people who demanded that you do things that didn't resonate with you, that didn't feel right?

CL: No. When I couldn't sing it this way or that way, I spoke with them always.

NG: You were very blessed. But also, you're very flexible, I imagine, and adaptable.

CL: Of course. Because I think each conductor has idea how he wants to do this piece. So, one is like this, one is like this, one is like this. But if they are good conductors, their concept is always good. I had in some score, I don't know where it was, in one phrase I had I have written pianissimo, mezzo forte, staccato, legato: all the different ideas from the conductors how they wanted it. But for each conductor's concept, it was right. So I adjusted. I had no character, in other words. Because I saw it is his intention to do a work like this. Of course, it was also good.

NG: And you understood what he was looking for.

CL: *Ja*, I understood how he wanted to do the piece, no?

NG: You sang a lot of roles that were very, very difficult. I mean, even for you, I would imagine Leonore of Fidelio was ... that's not a picnic. That's not easy.

CL: No, no, this was my child of sorrow.

NG: To me it's one of your greatest . . . it's the greatest recording of all of that opera, with Klemperer.

CL: It is good, yes. My mother sang Fidelio with Karajan when I was eight years old. I love this opera. I wanted always to sing it. I wanted always to sing the aria, the big aria. And I screamed it at home. Loud, always. I was so unhappy that I'm not a soprano and I couldn't sing the high notes and it was terrible. Then I said, once in my lifetime to sing Fidelio, and then I can die. Then came this offer from Klemperer to sing it on the record. Oh, it was fantastic. Because Klemperer was sick, he could do only two hours a day.

NG: That was good for you, too.

CL: *Ja.* Then in the late afternoon we had rehearsal on the piano in the house of Legge/Schwarzkopf, and the next day, it was at eleven or so, we had to sing two hours. We were always in good voice, of course.

Then came Karajan, who wanted it from me here in Vienna. When I sang it here, I thought, "And now I will die." Really because it was so my wish to sing this role. Because of the humanity of this opera and because it is Beethoven. And then with the Quartet in the first act, I thought I really could now die.

I sang it only with Klemperer, Karajan, and Böhm. And then came Knappersbusch. I sang with him in the concert the scene and end of Isolde. This was a time where people thought I could be a high dramatic soprano. It was impossible; it was not possible. But he wanted to conduct Fidelio with me. I didn't: no. He would be too slow for me.

NG: And you knew that he wouldn't adapt.

CL: No, no. I also sang one aria of Lady Macbeth in Maggio Musicale with, what is his name? Wonderful conductor: long, tall man, beautiful.

NG: Guilini? A wonderful conductor.

CL: Very catholic, *ja*. And he had to conduct this Macbeth. I didn't do it because I couldn't sing the last high note in pianissimo: a high D flat. I sing all the time high D flat, but not in the aria. I couldn't sing it. And here [in Vienna] I sang it [the aria] a little bit lower, but I knew in Italy, no. Impossible.

NG: In Italy it had to be in the original key.

CL: So, I was always . . . prudent.

NG: Did you work with Solti?

CL: Ach, a lot. I hated him. You know why?

NG: Why?

CL: When he gave the direction to start to sing, he did this [she gestured a violent pointing gesture]. And he did this. I couldn't look to him. Terrible. I couldn't look at Böhm either. I say to him, "I cannot sing when I look to you." He said to me, "But you sing always right." I said, "I know the music."

NG: You mean the upbeat was violent and it made you nervous?

CL: No, not violent. He was hectic. I love more . . .

NG: Round, calm gestures.

CL: Then it's also for a singer better to sing. It is the same if you give a trumpet a hectic upbeat.

NG: Exactly. You have to offer an invitation.

CL: Yes, always. And Solti was terrible. I had my first bursting capillaries because of him. It was Kundry. *Ja*, Kundry. The screaming of Kundry. Three hours. Only screaming. "Too high, too low, not enough." Three hours. I went home and it was terrible. Then the next day . . .

NG: They should have hired someone to do the screams for you.

CL: Here, in Vienna, I never screamed. It was always somebody else doing it for me. No, no: I screamed as Kundry. I didn't scream as Klytemnestra behind the scene. No.

NG: Speaking of stage screams, did you sing Sieglinde?

CL: No. This was not my part. I was Fricka. I had a wonderful stage director in Paris. He wanted to have a real horse on the stage, with a tail, and so he got it. But stuffed, not real, and the entire scenery was sacks of sand.

I had a wonderful costume, blue big cape, and my wig had Aries horns. Aries, *ja*? I had on my wonderful cape and two sheep. But there were the sacks of sand. *Ja*, but now with the sand sacks, I had to lift up the costume with the sheep?

I came onstage, and I did this, and the whole audience laughed. This was the only one time in my career I could say, this staging concept was really unnecessary. And it was the time of Rolf Lieberman, when he was in Paris, director. And he canceled the other two Siegfried and Götterdämmerung, he canceled. They were all paid, but he didn't want any more from this stage director.

NG: Did you ever say to a stage director, "I can't do this. This is not going to work"?

CL: I'm not that type of woman, no.

NG: You'd always try.

CL: *Ja.* And if something disturbs me, I tell them, "It disturbs me because . . ." I explain. I don't say "never." I don't do it.

NG: You're not Maria Callas.

CL: Oh, no, no. It's unnecessary. Life is too short.

NG: Exactly. Why not be friendly?

CL: *Ja*, always when I explained why I couldn't do it . . . For example, I am for Fidelio not the heroic voice. I have a slender voice, so the orchestra must also play more piano. Then it's not the Beethoven they were used to, not the marble blocks. Karajan made them play with a smaller sound in order to balance with me, and he had bad critics, not me.

NG: You weren't a Brünnhilde type. You weren't a Gwyneth Jones.

CL: Right, I'm not Birgit Nilsson either. No, no. They adjusted because he [von Karajan] said, always, "We should sing as the orchestra plays, and the orchestra should listen to the singer, and play like the singer." This was very good, *ja*.

NG: Well, there's some conductors who know how to listen, and some orchestras that listen better than others.

CL: *Ja*, but this was the Vienna Philharmonic.

NG: The Metropolitan Orchestra, did they do well for you?

CL: Divine. Divine.

NG: How about the *bel canto* repertoire for you?

CL: Never.

NG: Well, you did sing Adalgisa?

CL: This was because an Italian mezzo-soprano was sick, canceled. And Walter Legge was at the Salzburg Festival, he said, "Can you sing next week Adalgisa?" I said, "What?"

NG: Next week?

CL: I had no idea what is normal. I never heard Bellini, never. So I got the music and I sang Adalgisa. I was asking the coach about Bellini style. And Callas said to me, "You imitate me, then it will be a little right."

NG: And was it?

CL: I couldn't imitate her because Norma had another character than Adalgisa. She is softer.

NG: More feminine, more vulnerable.

CL: But to sing the duets, of course, it was wonderful. Callas was a very, very nice, normal lady.

NG: That's what I always understood. Different than what the press made her out to be.

CL: I read once in a book, "A real Prima Donna has to have in a year seven scandals and seven successes."

NG: Well, you had the successes but not the scandals.

CL: I was too lazy! *Ja*, I'm too lazy for this, I couldn't. I had once a public relations man. He was angry that Walter Berry and I had no scandals, and he wouldn't continue working for us: He had nothing to write.

NG: Yes, but you always had success just by doing good work, for decades.

CL: *Ja*, but I was not so interesting.

NG: Tell me about being a soprano, because you sang some soprano roles.

CL: I am not a soprano. I tried to sing it.

NG: Why?

CL: Because I love in life, to overcome obstacles. This is my character. For example, the Marschallin in Der Rosenkavalier. I was in New York in a concert with Bernstein. I went backstage, and Bernstein said to me, "Here is my Marschallin!" I said, "I'm not Marschallin, I'm Octavian." He said, "No, no, with me you will sing Marschallin." My mother wrote . . . I was twenty-three years old, I sang for the very first time Octavian. I couldn't sing it. I thought after the second act the curtain could fall and never again. Okay, but the third act is not so important. But my mother wrote to me because she sang Octavian and not Marschallin. She wrote, "Now for Octavian, and later for Marschallin." This is the only score I kept. Everything else . . . When Lenny said I should sing Marschallin, ah, this was a fulfillment of my life. As it was with Fidelio. But I love the role through the first act, of course.

NG: Of course.

CL: Always when I sang Octavian I thought, "He is such a stupid boy. He understands nothing. What is this?" The only challenge in singing the Marschallin is the beginning of the trio. I never could sing it in pianissimo. It was impossible. I could sing it soft, but not pianissimo. Then once a conductor said to me, "CL, why don't you turn the back to the audience? Then it sounds softer, only for the beginning." This was very good! The sound came from a far-away place: only for the first part of the trio. Was a good idea.

NG: I always thought that Octavian is more difficult than the Marschallin. It's longer, and the tessitura is a little higher, no?

CL: *Ja*, the Marschallin is easier. It's more in the middle range. Octavian sings in the middle range, and suddenly high notes from nowhere. I hated this. It is difficult to sing, I think. But, of course, it is a joy to do it. It's fun. Very fun.

NG: In the same way, it always seems to me, studying the Verdi scores, that the mezzo roles have a slightly higher tessitura than the sopranos. Because they're always overwrought, and the sopranos are supposed to sound beautiful and easy all the time.

CL: This was, for example, when I sang Aida with Leontyne Price, she had the darker voice of the two of us. And I was Azucena to Price's Leonora: Terrible. I was terrible.

I had to darken my voice that I was the mezzo soprano and she was the soprano. But Legge told me this always, "If you have a light voice, you can sing your voice when you are singing alone, but when you are singing with someone who has a darker voice, you have to darken your voice." And I changed the color of my voice.

NG: Were there any problems with that? Did this compromise your tessitura in any way?

CL: No. I heard Price only by radio the last Aida in New York. She sang beautiful. Beautiful.

NG: It was her decision to stop.

CL: This is good. Wonderful. We have her in my ears and Donna Anna was beyond fantastic.

NG: You didn't sing Donna Anna, did you? You sang Elvira.

CL: Only on the record.

NG: Yes.

CL: But the aria [she began singing Mi tradì]?

NG: You sang it in a lower key than published.

CL: *Ja*, because Legge later found a score . . .

NG: That was one down a half step. Joyce diDonato sings it down the half step, too.

CL: Oh, I love her.

NG: Isn't she beautiful?

CL: Oh, she is fantastic. She's fantastic. *Ja*. I love her. She's the best in the moment, *ja*. The voice is so beautiful, and she is such a talent.

Iestyn Davies

Iestyn Davies is among the world's most celebrated countertenors. He sings at every major opera house and theater in the world. He was appointed Member of the Order of the British Empire (MBE) in the 2017 New Year Honors for services to music. In the following wide-ranging interview, he shares his thoughts on role preparation, particularly in relation to Baroque opera repertoire, rehearsal comportment, and professionalism.

Neal Goren: How do you begin to develop a character when learning a new role?

Iestyn Davies: Approaching character, I would say, you try everything you can, come at it from every angle. And then, you make this big casserole of ideas. But you don't put it in the oven until you get to the staging rehearsals.

NG: You can't cook it just yet. You think about possibilities of what you want, what the character might be trying to communicate? And then, you try them on for size, see what you think is appropriate, but keep it fluid until you get into a notion of what the stage director has in mind?

ID: In Handel, where you have a lot to sing, and a lot of the challenge is to try and present a vocally perfected version of Handel as well as some character, but not try to take one from the other. The challenge is to find that balance. But then, again, if you've gone so far into the character, it can help rather than hinder. It's just that you have to hold your hands up when you go to the first rehearsal, and say, "I don't really know anything" (but I secretly do). And the director will decide. And some directors let you explore what you've discovered.

NG: So you've considered a lot of things in your preparation, in other words?

ID: The longer you go on doing this job, the more you realize that if you don't put much in, you're going to find it really boring after a while. And it's quite easy, at the beginning of your career, to just focus on the singing, because people just want to hear your voice. I think that if you put a lot more into the process of learning the role beforehand, then, at moments of crisis in rehearsal, where the director may not know where things are going, you have a contribution, and you can say, "Well, I've actually thought about this." And, surprise! A singer's thought about something, and it can help.

NG: I often say that famous singers run the risk of becoming caricatures of themselves, of what they think made them famous in the first place. And they just keep on repeating that, instead of trying new things and experimenting.

ID: It's that change blindness. You live with your voice every day, so you don't hear the way it changes to other people. In the same way, until we look at photographs of ourselves twenty years ago, you don't realize how much you've aged, or matured, whichever way you like to look at it.

NG: Are you saying that it's a good thing to feel like you're reinventing yourself all the time, and reinventing the score every time you pick it up, or every day that you're singing it?

ID: Yeah, well, not even reinventing. I think, if you're living in the moment and you're reacting, you pick something up. And especially something you've considered before in the preparation.

I like being prodded by a good stage director to be the actor rather than the singer. And I think that's what makes it interesting.

That's when the music is almost not in the background; but it's there supporting what you're doing as an actor. But that rarely happens in opera.

I remember preparing Oberon, a short role for which I had quite a lot of time on my hands, so I sat down and I thought: "I'm going to really think like a Shakespearean actor. I'm going to think about Oberon." Which is all very well, but you're not doing Shakespeare's play, you're doing Britten's reduction of it. Plus, the composer has already kind of straitjacketed you by putting music around what he says.

NG: He's made his decisions that you must honor and justify.

ID: Yes, there's some degree of interpretation, but often that's in a much bigger thing, limited by the set and with the setting. We singers are always caught between a rock and a hard place. If you're doing a recital, you can decide everything for yourself because you're in charge, but if you're performing in an opera, I find that it's not until you're in your costume and you're on stage when you might realize: "Ah! My character, actually, is not necessarily all about me. I now see how Handel wrote this aria to be a springboard for the next person to sing. It serves a larger function."

Let's go back to what we were saying about singers becoming parodies of themselves. You must keep yourself interested in the profession. We're doing something which people are paying to come and watch, and the idea of performance is that you're giving other people an emotional reaction and pleasure. To keep it alive, you have to maintain a little equity in that deal. Which is that you still own a lot of the enjoyment out of this, you still have to feel mentally stimulated by what you're doing; and that comes from investigating characters and redoing things in a different way.

With us, all that kind of work is in private. We only get paid and we only get recognized for what happens on stage. Sitting at home on your own and learning music, that's often when you are feeling the most creative. And when you go on stage it's the least creative, because you've already created the thing in rehearsal, and on stage you embody it and you live it. You're never quite making something new in opera. Which is why I love recitals, because the recitals are a chance ... You are the director, you're the conductor, you're the singer; you're all those things at once.

NG: You, as a performer, can only achieve your artistic goals if your technique works for you and you don't have to think about it. Your technique can allow you to facilitate different aspects of what you might want, what your character might be communicating in any one moment. But the one thing that you don't want the audience to see is that you're vacant.

ID: Yeah. If the lights are on and nobody's in. Realistic acting is really hard ... because there's only so far you can go with a certain style.

NG: A lot further in Handel than in nineteenth-century music!

ID: The emotions and the psychological drama that's going on in Handel operas are as relevant today as they were then; it's just presented in a different way.

NG: So what about specificity versus generalized emotion or communication?

ID: In what sense?

NG: I mean, when you have one of these arias that goes pages and pages, are you specific with yourself as to what you're trying to communicate in this phrase, versus what you're trying to communicate in that phrase? Or is it just—

ID: Well, again, that can be dictated by what's happening on the set. In an opera full of props or in a real setting, the set will dictate a lot. While you might have a specific reason to sing something, you're picking up whatever, it's a knife, or something.

It's almost as if, with Handel, the music is like a spell that captures the character at the time. You can think about it, you can put in all these extra things, but the composer, there, does own you slightly.

And then there are those, "Oh my God!" moments. And it's always the one that people go, "Oh, that aria you sang at the end of the first act was really good." And that was the moment when I didn't do anything: In the staging, I literally got beaten over the head, covered in blood, and stood there, and that was enough. I then said to myself, "Now, just listen to the music," without it becoming park-and-bark. What I didn't do was surrender myself to nineteenth-century opera: standing there with my arms out and finding a good position on that stage. I just had to be slightly limp and about to die, and just sing this beautiful aria. That sort of sort of symbiosis between the singing and the acting works.

It's, like, at this particular moment, as long as you're living in the moment and being sincere to what Handel has written in terms of the music, that will be as powerful as it can be. Anything else, histrionic, can kind of take away from the music, but that's the problem.

So it's a really fine balancing act with Baroque opera, I think. It's knowing when to realize that you are subordinate there. And you do find it in contemporary music of course, but it's so much more obvious there, when you're doing something out of line.

NG: So do you look at the score and say, so why did he do it this way?

ID: Yeah. Well, I think you have to acknowledge that yes, Handel could only write in a certain way because of the eighteenth century. But at the same time, he's obviously a super-intelligent, genius guy. You just have to imagine that it's possible that everything he wrote was for a very psychological reason. That's what you learn from working with living composers: That they write very specific things because it matters to them, rather than they just need to fill a quarto of pages.

NG: Do you have more opportunity for interpretation in recitative: secco recitative?

ID: Yeah, well, recitative is interesting, because that is where, I think, with stuff like Handel, there's a lot more detail that you can bring to a character.

The recitative doesn't inform you, but you can inform the audience. You can use that as a tool to show the audience. Because there's a lot more freedom in the recitative if the conductor and the director allow it.

In the recit, it's the speed of delivery and often the silences which tell you stuff. If I were directing, I would get two characters, if they were speaking to each other, to actually speak the scene before: to learn what those things would sound like, how you would react at normal speed. It's so easy to act to the speed of the music, then people don't react at all. They stand still until they have to sing, or they walk slowly when the music is slow, and things like that.

But I think, on one level, beyond finding that reason to say something, one can also consider methods of delivery: over-enunciating, doing something with the color of the vowel: All those kind of things show some sort of intent every time you say something. It will sound spontaneous; it should sound like it's coming from a reaction to something at that particular moment.

NG: Can we discuss ornamenting the repeat in a da capo aria?

ID: That's where looking into characters really does become the modern approach of thinking about the characters as you would with a play. It helps, because you can ask yourself: "What kind of ornamentation is going to bring something out in the character?" rather than just in the musical sense. I think that the predominant concern about ornamentation has largely been strictly musical, which doesn't really necessarily serve what's going on.

The director Barrie Kosky is always saying, "Use your words as weapons." When you're standing on stage with another character, everything you say is the only thing that's being said at that moment. We can talk about what it means, we can talk about the relationships, we can talk about back-stories, we can talk about what's happening in the future, but at that particular moment those characters are reacting to each other. Acting is reacting. When you hear somebody say something in real life, you have a reaction, even if it's silence. If somebody's saying something, that must be the most important thing that's happening at that particular time.

"Use your words as weapons." Weapon, in the sense that it provokes, rather than it hurts. It can hurt, but it can also provoke laughter, or it can provoke love . . .

NG: Let me just finish up with one question that sort of feels obligatory: As you approach a new score, do you approach it with the spirit of inquiry?

ID: I have notebooks and markings in scores where I've really gone into something in detail . . . Because actually, I think, one of the quickest ways to memorize something is to really get inside it, find the skeleton of how the composer wrote it, see where the harmony is, look at the text, and then suddenly when you go, "Okay, I'm going to close the book and sing the first two phrases," and they're already there, because you've made so many emotional references. Emotion goes to the amygdala, which goes into the hippocampus, which creates memory. If your memory is formed by emotional contact, you remember everything much quicker.

When we go on stage and have props, and people, you remember everything. Then you get to the Sitzprobe with the orchestra, and you take all that away, you're like, "I can't remember how it goes!"

The spirit of inquiry aids in learning the score. Those things really, really help with the memorization. If you turn up loving your music, that's fine, but the expectation is that you come to the first rehearsal with it completely memorized as well. And to me that seems the wrong way about everything, but it is the gold standard of professionalism.

Getting to the point of memorizing your music, you've already done the inquiry. I find the quickest way of learning is applying an inquisitive mind, and then forgetting everything as much as possible, then memorize like a robot, and finally re-energize it again with questioning.

Jonas Kaufmann

Tenor **Jonas Kaufmann** (b. 1969) is perhaps the most-sought-after tenor in the world. He sings virtually the entire lyric, spinto, and lighter dramatic repertoire in all of the major opera houses in the world.

Neal Goren: My first question is, do you begin with the text or the music when you start learning a new role?

Jonas Kaufmann: It depends. When I do *Lied*, which is mostly based on poems, I start with the text and then go to the music. And with opera, it's different because, very often, it's highly emotional music and quite modest-quality texts. So, if you only go by the text to build your character, it's not really very satisfying. That's why I think for opera, the combination of both makes more sense.

You see, with opera, the music provides a general mood, but rarely a detailed or specific emotional interpretation. In the music of an opera the composer has already made his interpretation of the text. And if you don't comply with that interpretation or find a very good reason to go against it, you will fight against the music for the rest of your performances. If you don't agree with the interpretation that the composer has given you, it's difficult to get away with another. Even within the composer's interpretation of the text, there's still a million possibilities to interpret.

And I try to find the source material. You have the obvious ones like *La dame aux Camélias* or the *Carmen* from Mérimée, or all the Schiller and Shakespeare plays which ultimately became operas. If you have all the information that the source material provides, you see there is obviously much more than the few things that end up in the opera. Even Wagner presents the short version of the source material. As an actor, you put every bit of information you have from the source material into your character. It helps enormously if you know things that the author or the composer may not have known. It makes it much easier to slip into this character and to understand its difficulties, which gave rise to all the emotions that we hear in the music.

Therefore, I think that knowledge of the source material is perhaps more important maybe than the text itself. And it also helps if you read what the other characters are doing. It often happens that there are singers on stage that have no clue what happens in the scenes they're not in. No, I'm not joking; this can't work. We must work hand in hand in the ensemble. And if someone just goes in a different direction because he doesn't know what we're all aiming for, it's just no help, let's say.

NG: Yes. So then, what is the role of the director in helping you develop your interpretation or your character?

JK: Interesting question. You know I'm married to a director: careful now! No, I think it's very simple. Of course, opera directors and theater directors are different things. Because, as I said, in opera we do have to work within the composer's interpretation of the text. And we cannot just cut it, shorten it, change it, turn it upside down; You can't change a scene order, you can't whisper or scream where the orchestra plays at a different volume. And also, the rhythm. You can't just make a pause whenever you want. When there is music running through, there's no way that you say, oh, wait a minute, I think I have to let this phrase sit a little longer before I continue.

These are facts that an opera director has to understand and accept. In earlier operas like in Mozart's, or even still in Rossini, where you have recits and one number following the other, you have little bit more flexibility. But in the later operas, whether it's Verdi or Puccini or Wagner and so on, there's no chance. Once the train starts, it just keeps rolling. And this is something theater directors often underestimate: how precise the timeline is already fixed. But it is also an advantage, because it saves you a lot of rehearsal time. The whole process that you have in theater of brainstorming is irrelevant in opera: Well, let's try this. No, maybe let's try that. I mean reading the text over and over again until it comes to you that it's maybe a good idea to do that very soft or do that very fast. Whatever.

But in opera, on the other hand, you have to be on that train. And in an ideal world, you also have to support what the composer has written. The opera director must fight for the music and not against it. He must completely trust the power and the magic of the music. I always try to tell young directors that they need to come extremely prepared, first, because of that timeline that exists that they cannot violate. And second, because, unfortunately, we still have singers who hardly remember their own texts, who have no idea about what was going on around them and are so focused on hitting the high notes that they are unable to do much more than that. And you still have to find a way to keep them in the boat and not make it obvious at all. You have to give them things to do. It is great if you have singers who love to act, and who have made up their mind, and know their part inside out, have thought about the text, have thought about their personal interpretation, and do it just as actors do. Then the director can be an arbiter sitting in the audience who says, "I want more of that. I want less of this. And this, I don't understand, you have to find something else." But it often happens that the singers stand there and say, "So, what's next? What shall I do? Is it good if I stand here for the first verse? And do I really need to move for the next one? It's uncomfortable." The opera director must find a way to make the singers happy and make themselves happy at the same time.

In rehearsal, stage directors often ask me, "Have you done this role before?" "Yes." "What did you do here? Just do what you always did." And this is just wrong. And of course, there are directors who bring a great new interpretation and new ideas to a piece without destroying it, without harming it in any way. On the contrary, by widening the horizon it makes you realize, "Oh wow, I never thought about this. I've performed the piece so many times, but your interpretation actually gives us a new perspective and sharpens the situation and the problems."

NG: Those are the creative directors.

JK: Yes. But it's not very often the case. I have no general advice to offer young opera directors other than you have to be prepared and respect the piece. The music will help you pull it off. If you work against the music, the music will work against you. The music will win.

NG: You had said a few minutes earlier that it's ideal when other singers come to rehearsal having made up their minds about their character. How fixed can that characterization be when you're going to work with a director and a conductor who may have different ideas?

JK: True. Well, it can. I mean, of course, I'm maybe in a minority that can get away with opposing ideas. My advice to singers is, don't just criticize if you don't agree with what you've been asked to do. Bring an alternative. If you say, "How about this?" in 99 percent of the cases, they will buy it. It's always better to have someone who is convinced what he's doing on stage than someone who performs every requested gesture without agreeing. Many, many years ago, in one of my very first productions, the director said an interesting thing to me. He said, "Well, for me, an ideal scenario is that I have a film of the opera in my head, and you have a film of it in your head. And all we have to do is to cut it and make a version that we're all satisfied with." And this is brilliant, because it shows that each of us is responsible for coming with his own conception. And it always has to be a compromise in an ideal world. Because we'll never agree on everything. Everyone needs to be represented in it, or at least the people who are interested in being represented. And that is, I think, a very good way of approaching a production.

NG: So a good director allows the cast to collaborate to make a production?

JK: Of course. When a director has a very extreme concept for the production, it's always a great idea to come and talk about it before rehearsals begin and not just show up on the first day and say, "Oh, and by the way, I've turned the whole story upside down." That helps a lot if the director is willing to make compromises and give the signal that not everything is fixed in concrete. Oh, also, with the conductor. The day of the tyrant conductor is past. Now we try to build together and try to support together.

On the other extreme, there was a time where the conductor was only there to keep things together and serve the singers. But this is also not good. If you give singers too much freedom, it doesn't help. It's also the responsibility of the conductor to present an opera all in one style. And this is impossible with one singer all the time schlepping and doing one fermata after the other and another who is always rushing. The opera has to be in, more or less, the same style or the same—

NG: —overarching concept.

JK: Yeah. That said, I feel strongly that you have to negotiate, and you have to talk. A conductor cannot just say, "This is it: take it or leave it."

NG: One hopes that everyone is there to serve the music.

JK: Basically, yes. That would be absolutely enough if we all believe that we tried to make the music as good as possible, to help the music. That's all we need.

NG: I have one last question, which is, when you return to a role in a new production that you've already performed, do you start the process anew from the beginning, or do you just continue on with what you've done before?

JK: Well, vocally, I would say I continue. That is unless I've learned it differently or wrong, in which case it's a good chance for me to reconsider and once and forever get it right. But interpretation-wise, I think I, not only for a new production, I start fresh to allow change and growth. I have friends and fans that follow me around who try to see two or three performances. They say it's interesting how much changes in the course of a run, or from production to production. Because exploration and examination are a constant process; it's always something new.

And it's the same in *Lied* recital. When we do a *Lied* tour with the same concert program eight or ten times with the same pianist, why would we just do exactly the same thing over and over again? That would be tedious. So we try to really start from scratch each and every time. And in the case of an opera, it's the same world, in that the character has the same problem every performance. And the same relationships to the others. But per-haps because I stand up differently or I understand something new about whatever is happening to my character, it results in a slightly new interpretation. It may end up very similar, obvi-ously. But it is different because it just felt slightly different. And sometimes I'm on stage, and I perform a role that I have done lots of times and I suddenly think, "But this is it. Now, I understand. Maybe it's because he's . . ."

I mean, the words may strike me as something completely different than before. Because this phrase is the key phrase. Because with this realization, it makes the whole third act look differently. And it's fantastic. Because if you don't keep looking, if you don't keep trying and searching, you would end up in a rou-tine that is boring for yourself. And unfortunately, sooner or later, boring for the audience as well. Because they've heard it. They've heard the Kaufman Cavaradossi, or whatever. And it's going to be the same one over and over again. And I think that's wrong.

And it's that crucial for me that when I record something, I give all my heart. And when they send me the tapes, two months later, I think, "Oh God, I should have done it completely differently." Because I'm already—

NG: A different person.

JK: Of course, again, we're talking about a difference that's only slightly perceptible to the audience. A new production of a familiar role allows me to make a step forward interpretively. In the interim between the new production and the last, I've had more experience in life, and I realize that I should probably have done things slightly differently the first time. It's exciting, because this is what keeps me going. And it keeps this whole business extremely attractive in my view. It could be very boring doing the same things over and over. Looking at the character anew can make it fresh again.

NG: So you allow your characters to evolve and grow.

JK: Of course, they grow. Exactly. And usually, they grow deeper and deeper and, in many cases, darker and darker. As you grow older, you lose your innocence regarding some roles and discover other aspects to your character, where you formerly may have only seen one. It's difficult to not see the double sense in certain things.

I'm certainly not complaining.

NG: Oh, no. Of course not. Well, I thank you so much. This has been very enlightening.

Davóne Tines

Bass-baritone **Davóne Tines** is one of the world's most-sought-after singers of contemporary music. He is a graduate of Harvard University and of the Juilliard School. In the following interview, we learn that his process in constructing a character for music of our time requires some additional steps from that of constructing a character for music of the standard period.

Neal Goren: As someone who has a lot of experience both in standard repertoire and in contemporary music, I want to talk to you about your process in constructing a character. Do you approach it differently in contemporary music? Is it a different process than it is for your standard repertoire?

Davóne Tines: Yes and no. So I really do enjoy being a part of the process of making a new thing. I love that process because it seems like the impetus is always clear, and there's a lot of gal-vanized energy around why something is happening. I love that that *why* is always a present question in the team's mind, col-lectively. And that filters into kind of how I am considering the thing personally. So then, why are we bringing this person to life? Why is this person here? And then, more specifically, after the why is a bit clearer, then we'll get to know the who.

So, for instance, in John Adams's *Girls of the Golden West*, I created the role of Ned Peters, who is a conglomerate of a lot of different things. It is partly James Williams, who was an escaped slave. He literally walked out of slavery when he was thirteen by being kind of thoughtful. Every time he got caught, he said, "Oh, I belong to the master over there." Then he'd walk over there, and then he'd say, "Oh, I belong to the master over there." And slowly, miles by miles, he made his way west. And had a really amazing life of becoming a cowboy, and having a lot of different trades, and having a stagecoach business, and getting to know Native Americans. There's a really beautiful, his own memoir and then some other things that were written about him. So, he, along with Frederick Douglass and a fiddler-slave called Paganini Ned, was the basis of my character, Ned Peters.

NG: So are you saying, at least in this opera, you start with the source material?

DT: Mm-hmm (affirmative). And having done a number of works with Peter Sellars, he does literal mountains of research. So if you visit with him, he can give you maybe the ten books that your role is pulled from. And so, reading some of these first-hand accounts, and reading the Douglass speeches and getting to know these people more, you get a picture of their personalities. You kind of make a composite, and you see what resonates within yourself that you can utilize as a real . . . You have the template before you of what the emotion is, and you have to find some-thing true within yourself in order to fill that.

NG: So is that before you've even taken a look at the texts that you're going to be singing?

DT: No, it's in conjunction. Because as a matter of efficiency, you need to know a little bit of where you're going, right?

NG: Right.

DT: So an aria has a certain text, and the story has a certain arc. In my learning process, specifically, for all things, contemporary and old, I really like to work from the outside in. So for instance, when I learned Adams's *El Niño*, that was one of my first large roles that I performed internationally. So, it was John Adams's seventieth birthday celebration that went on for about a year, and so his music was programmed a lot of places. And after seeing me in Matt AuCoin's *Crossing*, he asked me to do *El Niño*, and it was a huge task. It's a long piece. It's very complicated. Lots of time signature and rhythmic things, and maybe melodic lines that don't seem regular, although there is a logic, of course. But I just listened to the piece for a year before looking at the score. A year, just to build in my mind what the arc was. So I had kind of the luxury of it being one of my first major things, having two and a half years out.

NG: So you first sort of jumped in to get the style to become part of you?

DT: Yes. It was the only thing I listened to in the car for like a year.

NG: Goodness!

DT: Yeah, listening to the style, starting to understand the main points of the story, understanding how my particular role fit into that structure. And then, once you got the big chunks down, you can move into what the arias are separately, and how they juxtapose with each other, or how they progress in the piece. So, you know what you're going for and what you have to reserve yourself for, or what have you. But rhythmically, it sounds impossible. The first time you hear it, you go, "I could never do that. How does it work?" And it's in 2/2, and it's a lot of eighth notes that are basically super-fast 16th notes. And so, of course you pull it down, slow it exactly down. But in the working outside in, you understand the larger phrases and how they block out, and then you understand how it fits together. All of this filigree filler, but beautiful movement line, that it's really in a big three.

And when you can think in these bigger ways, then you move forward in, a little more in, and then you realize the coloratura is just an expansion on a much simpler line of quarter notes. And then, so in terms of preparing this dramatically, yeah, it's the time where this character who is kind of a God voice or an every being, says that God will become embodied and shake the heavens apart. And, of course, that's from the largest boulders of the tectonic plates to the tiny pebbles. So, you get all of that in the macro rhythm: I really do appreciate this idea of getting the larger picture, so you know where you're going, and then working inward. And in that way, if it's a clear line into the center, all of the choices are honest to what the larger picture is.

NG: Do you embark on your learning a new score with the spirit of sort of inquiry, as to why is he putting this here, and why is he doing this here?

DT: Oh, yes. Yeah, definitely.

NG: Do you start with the text and then go to the music later?

DT: Yeah.

NG: So, when you're looking at the texts, do you say, "How would I set that?" Or "How do I think it will be set musically?"

DT: You read the text, but in wanting to be efficient, you do take on some sort of understanding or perspective of the composer's language, and that works across the board, right? Bach on up, or back even. And you learn their language, you try to understand their perspectives, so that when you go to learn something, you can be a bit efficient and have a bit of a vocabulary for why they made certain choices. For example, the goal [of both John Adams and Matt AuCoin] is communication. The goal is to illuminate human speech as if it were to be dramatized, or put in a way that is more consumable. Because I mean, if anything is sung to someone, they're going to receive it in a more complex way than if you just speak it to them. That's why we do opera.

NG: Right.

DT: And that's the trick, right? The trick is for the audience to not understand that you are [counting and subdividing], just seeming to say it as if it flows out. But just the way that Matt [AuCoin] hears in his mathematical mind, he has set it. And that's what it is.

NG: So, did you have to deduce his goal yourself, or did he actually explain that it you clearly?

DT: Oh, he made himself clear by being extremely upset in rehearsal.

DT: And when it comes to the music of [Kaija] Saariaho ...

NG: It's all about the color.

DT: You're exactly right. Because at the end of the day ... Because she'll go through the painstaking effort of putting all this [detail] in, but so much in rehearsal she says, "You know what, that's beautiful. It's beautiful. Just do naturally." Whereas some other composers are much more exacting ...

NG: Like Matt.

DT: Yes, yes.

NG: Well, actually, I now want to summarize a little bit: that you'll start out from the text after immersing yourself in the composer's language.

DT: Yes.

NG: And then, if there are source materials, you'll go and you'll sort of flesh out what you have decided it is you're trying to express.

DT: Exactly.

NG: Then you'll go and look to the music.

DT: And the psychology.

NG: Yes. And then you'll go to the music and see how they align.

CHAPTER 21

DT: How they align, or don't, sometimes.

NG: Don't align, and that's when it becomes particularly interesting.

DT: At that point you then sort of question why . . .

A Few Closing Thoughts

Afterword

Every aspect of this book grew from my reverence for the music. Assuming that you share this reverence, the methodology I have advocated will result in a joyful process of discovery that will directly impact your performances. While there is no guarantee that this will result in more or better singing gigs, it is sure to enrich your interpretations and presentations and make you a more interesting artist and interpreter.

You may have noted in the interview section that not all of the represented singer-actors practice what I have preached. With a busy schedule, it is often necessary to streamline the learning process. Another fact that arose is that there is a danger of entering rehearsals with your character too fully formed in your mind. In professional situations (versus auditions), you must remain open and flexible at all times.

Intelligent inquiry is the key to artistic self-empowerment. Require it of yourself! It will pay off in untold ways.

References

Chapter 1
1   Scotto, Renata, *More Than a Diva,* Doubleday, 1984, 141.

Chapter 4
1   Newman, Sandra, "The Lost Art of the Manly Weep," Aeon newsletter online, June 5, 2018.
2   Elliott, Martha, *So You Want to Sing Early Music: A Guide for Performers,* Rowman & Littlefield, 2019.
3   Haynes, Bruce, *A History of Performing Pitch: The Story of 'A',* Scarecrow Press, 2002.
4   Baird, Julianne C., translator and editor, *Introduction to the Art of Singing by Johann Friedrich Agricola,* Cambridge University Press, 1995.
5   Ibid., p. 28.
6   Ibid., p. 32.
7   Couperin, Francois, "*L'art de toucher le clavecin*" (English title: *The Art of Playing the Harpsichord*), 1716, rev. 1717. (Many editions available.)
8   Elliott, Martha, *Singing in Style,* Yale University Press, 2006, p. 41.
9   Harnoncourt, Nicholas, *Baroque Music Today: Music as Speech,* Amadeus Press, 1988, p. 16.
10   See "The Myth of Whiteness in Classical Sculpture" by Margaret Talbot, *The New Yorker* magazine, October 29, 2018.
11   Kerman, Joseph, *Opera as Drama,* Knopf, 1956, p. 292.
12   Kloiber, Rudolf, Wulf Konold, and Robert Maschka, *Handbuch der Oper (9th ed.),* Kassel: Bärenreiter, 2002.
13   Osborne, Charles, *Letters of Giuseppe Verdi,* Gollancz, 1971, pp. 36–37.
14   Ibid., p. 113.
15   Ibid., p. 60.
16   Ibid., p. 175.
17   Weiner, Marc A., *Richard Wagner and the Anti-Semitic Imagination,* University of Nebraska Press, 1995, pp. 103–53.
18   "Wagner and Bel Canto" by Jens Malte Fischer, *The Opera Quarterly,* Volume 11, Issue 4, 1995, pp. 53–58.
19   Scott, Michael, *The Record of Great Singing to 1914,* Scribner, 1977, p. 103.

Chapter 5
1 Bernac, Pierre, *The Interpretation of French Song,* Gollancz, 1978, pp. 3 and 5.
2 Ibid., p. 5.
3 Teyte, Maggie, *Star at the Door*, Putnam, 1958, p. 57.

Chapter 10
1 From a February 4, 2017, televised interview with Harvey Sachs.

Chapter 12
1 Ardoin, John, *Callas: The Art and the Life*, Holt, Rinehart and Winston, 1974, p. 12.
2 From Callas interviews with Edward Downes for Met opera intermission (December 30, 1967, and January 13, 1968).
3 Ardoin, pp. 13–14.
4 "Maria Callas talks about Wagner and *bel canto*," YouTube.
5 From Callas interviews with Edward Downes for Met opera intermission (December 30, 1967, and January 13, 1968).

Index

About the Author

Conductor **Neal Goren** was the founder and artistic director of Gotham Chamber Opera, which popularized and legitimized the formerly ignored genre of chamber opera, which has now attained respect equal to the pillars of the of the operatic repertoire. In its fifteen years of existence, Goren conducted all of Gotham's twenty-seven productions, which included the world premieres by Nico Muhly's *Dark Sisters* and Lembit Beecher's *I have no stories to tell you*; and the U.S. stage premieres of works by Kaija Saariaho, Toshio Hosokowa, Bohuslav Martinu, and Xavier Montsalvatge. Gotham's production often featured unexpected elements, such as site-specific presentations in locales thematically related to the operas, such as Cavalli's *Eliogabalo* presented in the Box, a louche Manhattan night club; Haydn's *Il mondo della luna*, presented in the Hayden Planetarium of the American Museum of Natural History; and Daniel Catan's *La hija de Rappaccini*, presented in the Rose Garden of the Brooklyn Botanical Garden and the Greystone Manor Gardens in Beverly Hills, California. Other Gotham productions were staged by directors best known for their work in other artistic genres, such as choreographers Mark Morris, Karole Armitage, David Parsons, and Luca Veggetti; Broadway directors Moisès Kaufman and Rebecca Taichman, and puppeteer Basil Twist. Other Gotham productions featured sets by internationally celebrated visual artists Georg Baselitz and Vera Lutter.

Goren's other conducting credits include *Die Zauberflöte* for New York City Opera and the Trentino Festival (Italy), *Dark Sisters* by Nico Muhly (European premiere) for Trentino Festival and for Opera Philadelphia; *Transformations* by Conrad Susa, for San Francisco Opera Center; *Mila* by Eli Marshall (world premiere) for Asia Society of Hong Kong and additional performances in New York and San Francisco; and *Anaïs Nin* and *Odysseus' Women* by Louis Andriessen (U.S. premiere) for Center for Contemporary Opera.

A much sought-after recital accompanist, Goren was a protétgé of Geoffrey Parsons and has concertized extensively with Leontyne Price, Kathleen Battle, Hei-Kyung Hong, Harolyn Blackwell, Hakan Hagegard, Lorraine Hunt Lieberson, Aprile Millo, Hermann Prey, among others. He is an associate professor at Mannes College, The New School for Music, where has served on the faculty since 1991. He is a frequent judge of national and international vocal and composers' competitions and is an annual featured guest on the Metropolitan Opera quiz.

Lightning Source UK Ltd.
Milton Keynes UK
UKHW020017071220
374732UK00006B/1340